T0149978

THE
LUMINARY

Journey

LESSONS FROM A VOLCANO IN CREATING
A HEALING CENTER AND BECOMING THE LEADER
YOU WERE BORN TO BE

DARSHAN MENDOZA

The LUMINARY *Journey*
LESSONS FROM A VOLCANO IN CREATING A HEALING CENTER AND
BECOMING THE LEADER YOU WERE BORN TO BE

Difference Press, Washington, D.C., USA

ISBN: 978–1–68309–246–9

Cover Design: Jennifer Stimson
Editing: Moriah Howell
Illustration: Alex Cabal
Author's photo courtesy of Darshan Mendoza

DP
DIFFERENCE
PRESS

To the very first teachers on my path
Mom and Dad
Zen and Juan
Salamat for showing me
what embodied spirituality feels like
down to the tissues of my heart
and
to the goddess Pelehonuamea who has shown me
how to walk through fire
and birth new worlds
from ashes

TABLE OF CONTENTS

A PRELUDE IN PARTS

Dear Luminary,

In my preparations of writing you this letter, I stumbled upon old notes from last year, when everything began to wobble, quake, and eventually turn into ashes on this island and simultaneously in my world. It was a transformation of all transformations — painful, confusing, liberating, surreal. I promised God and Tūtū Pele that if I lived through it mentally and emotionally, I would share the medicine that I could feel was brewing. I lived through it. I'm making good on my promise now.

May 1, 2018 — I got word that my mentor and dear friend Anutosh Foo had passed away. She was the first teacher we brought to our healing center who shared Systemic Family Constellation Work with our community. A hospice in Seattle who had a harpist and a pink poodle visiting her daily was the portal she chose for her ascension. She even told her sister Pat the exact date she would die, and she was right. She asked to be taken off of all her medications, as she wanted to be as lucid as possible through her passage. The folks at the hospice were so enamored with Anutosh, recognizing the living bodhisattva in their presence, teaching the exquisite grace of staying wide awake through every part of your life, including your death. This, amongst countless of wisdom teachings Anutosh shared with me in the potent year that I knew her, was an integral lesson I soon had to put to practice in a few days, when the Kīlauea volcano began to erupt here on the Big Island of Hawai'i.

Two weeks before she ascended from this earth plane, she left me a message saying, "Darshan, I wanted to share the most beautiful experience of dying. Call me back when you can." I thought, could she be possibly calling me from heaven? Her voice and tone were so typical of Anutosh, nonchalant with her beautiful Singaporean accent, making every word sound so musical and profound with a tinge of some hilarious anecdote waiting to come. You wouldn't have guessed cancer has taken over her bones and entire body. You wouldn't have guessed she was dying. Well, besides her saying she wanted to describe it to me over the phone.

I pulled the truck over at the Safeway parking lot in Hilo and I called her back right away.

She answered the phone and went right into what she needed to share. She was a woman on a mission; every word was intentional and focused. I realized that in the moment you know you're dying, you get laser sharp focused about everything you think, feel, express, and do. You live life so presently and aware. It was Anutosh being Anutosh — irreverent yet humble and deeply compassionate — amplified by death's urgency.

She wanted to share that moment she "slipped off her body like a cloak." She explained she was so transfixed on the beauty of these flowers that her friend had brought her from her garden. She suddenly felt herself slipping off and getting lighter and lighter and this feeling of intoxicating beauty and bliss filled her. I was bawling my eyes out as she spoke. There were several folks getting out of their cars and trucks in the parking lot who did their best to give me my space and look away. I didn't even register she was still alive and I really did believe she was calling me from heaven.

She then said, "but I realized my son was getting on a plane for Vietnam and I wanted to talk to him one last time and then I realized I still owed you my 1099s, so I came back to my body."

"Hold up, what?! Taxes, Anutosh?!" I mean that just brings the saying — the only guarantee in life is death and taxes — to a whole new level. She didn't want to leave anything unfinished, she said. There was so much I was learning from her about dying in that moment. We laughed and we cried and I personally felt I was talking to God or at least Her lady in waiting. The wisdom Anutosh shared on that call, I'm still integrating one year later and I suspect I will for the rest of my life.

In two weeks, Anutosh began her final ascension to heaven and simultaneously the earth here on the Big Island started splitting apart, fissures opened, and lava rivers began to flow. In many ways, we all began to ascend too. Heightened emergency alertness pumped through our nerves and veins as the lava pumped through the underground lava tubes. Many people needed to abruptly focus all of their energy intentionally and drop everything else that didn't have anything to do with survival. Packing belongings. Saying goodbye to homes, land, neighbors. Losing pets and farm animals. Gathering resources. Finding new shelter. Trying to get limited masks so they can breathe. Reconciling tremendous loss of dreams and plans with surrender.

A New Earth began to form beneath our feet. Volcanic ashes filled the air. Sulfuric particles embedded themselves into our hair, onto our skin and tongues. My mouth was coated in ashes, my lungs were processing the particles alongside the grief of so many things passing, burning too quickly for my heart to comprehend.

I found these notes and postings I had written during the first month of the eruption. Reading them again for the first time one year later is a time-traveling journey. I find myself wanting to reach out through the time machine and let myself back then know to tighten up her proverbial boot straps and put on her big girl panties and get ready. Life is about to take the strangest twists and turns. She will be heartbroken. She will leave her wife. She will get divorced. She will question her career. She will shed identities she's grown to love. She will lose friends. What she thought she knew for sure will burn to the ground. She will rise again though soon enough and like the Hopi Elder said, this will be the time to push herself into the rushing river, let go of the rocks, keep her head above the water, and her eyes open.

Anutosh's last call to me at that Safeway parking lot, describing her temporary death and return with such keen awareness was a memo from God that she brought back with her preparing me. At least that's how I received it. I would hear her voice and guidance often during the eruptions, guiding me from whatever realm she was journeying in. *Jump into this moment. It's happening, girlfriend. Complete everything that you have to. Don't leave anything unfinished. Pack up only your lessons and magic. Leave all other attachments behind. This is only the beginning of Earth's ascension. Oh Darshan, it is a magnificent unfolding! Keep your eyes wide open. And let it all burn.* And her signature line, *look upon everyone with kindness and ask to be looked upon with kindness too.* I knew from the first moment I picked her up from the Hilo Airport a year before her death that I was meeting my Guardian Angel in human form. I loved her immediately. Her first words to me when she got into the truck after the normal pleasantries were, "I'm dying. I have breast cancer. Don't tell anyone, please." From that moment on, I listened deeply to everything she wanted to share. I've continued to listen to her to this day. It feels like receiving voicemails from heaven.

The lava started erupting on May 3, 2018. I intuitively began documenting and collecting written letters, photographs, and even radio transcriptions. Something told me to pay a lot of attention to not only what was happening ecologically but also what was happening spiritually within our community and especially within me. I knew that someday these will be important artifacts to remember and that this is a monumental time in the history of this earth. Here are the notes I wrote down and collected...

May 4. 2018

Goodmorning Tūtū,

Mahalo nui for continuing to offer
us your fierce love and compassion.
She realigns you if you need it
She humbles you when you get a
little too high makamaka.
She amplifies whatever you are
denying within so you can clearly
see what may be blocking you from
living your best life.
She keeps the fire burning through
the storms of your life like a
lighthouse lighting your way.
And when it's necessary she sets
things on fire and cleans house.
You learn living next to such a
powerful force to listen and shift
when the first signs of stirring
begin
and welcome and surrender to her
lessons and initiations.

May 8. 2018

Visited Tūtū Pele at Kīlauea Crater tonight.
It's so still. It's so peaceful.
Like every element, plant and animal is holding space for Her.
An entire blanket of mist covers the crater from view.
It seems inappropriate to watch or look anyways.
It feels so grounded here. I hear a lot of sighs, deep breaths.
They bathe me and remind me to take deeper breaths myself.
Behind the mist I imagine a cauldron of medicine being stirred
— every whisper, feeling and prayer added in very intentionally.
Lonomakua arrives and it rains, a deliberate drizzle.
Everyone is coming across from all time
and space to pay their respect.
If you are a Seer, you'd probably see legions of souls.
The Wind shakes the Ohia Tree for a brief moment
igniting it into a dance.
Two nenes fly low peeking through the mist.
This is a sacred time.
And it seems all of existence knows it.

May 18. 2018

The lava took the homestead of April and Brad today. When I was a young yogini over a decade ago, this was the first home I lived in in Puna. I taught Kundalini Yoga for papayas and art. I was awakening in a really accelerated way and every day I would drive down Pohoiki and then the Red Road blasting Snatam's "Ong Namo" in my little spaceship Civic to get myself started before teaching the 6 a.m. class and I would, eighty percent of the time, cry at the beauty of this island — the rainforest canopy above the roads, the sunrise over the ocean, the magnificent bird songs — and I would just be overwhelmed by gratitude that I get to live, teach, heal and awaken here … to live amongst so much beauty on such primal earth.

All of the visions of this retreat center here in Volcano happened in that cabin. I fell in love for the first time on this island in that cabin. And I learned how to take care of chickens, how to clean a pond and the delight of eating fruits straight from the vine. I learned how to create a homestead. I learned how to summon fairies and notice them in their tree dwellings. I learned what made home magic — the life, love, generosity and aloha of the people who plant the seeds and nourish what grows and the laughter, tears and incredible feasts that arise from such a space and garden.

I connect to another timeline fifty years from now when vegetation and life regenerates itself on this lava, we may be walking these lands with our grandchildren and telling them about the life, home, people, and gardens that these trees now grow from.

My heart grieves for what no longer is there and the sudden loss that April and Brad are experiencing and my heart simultaneously celebrates the new life that will arise from this New Earth.

I was staying there years ago visiting from O'ahu when the Geothermal Plant started emitting poisonous gasses and we had to evacuate. I remember how angry I was at the negligence of this company and how they were destroying these lands.

Watching how the lava has been flowing, it seems to be heading straight there. And this is one of the homesteads in Her path.

We are all affected by the desecration of the earth — just like the plants, animals, rivers, oceans, and forests — we suffer the consequences and as the evolution of this planet accelerates there will be no human untouched, even if you are living pono in all ways.

This is our birthright now — to witness the old dying and birthing the new and the chaos and reordering that happens in between.

May 19. 2018

From Marianne Williamson's Love Letter to Hawai'i

Dear People of Hawaii,

I know it must be frightening to live in Hawaii right now.

I think of you constantly looking at the sky, checking the Internet for environmental updates, talking anxiously to friends and loved ones, telling tales, and comforting your children.

I hope you realize how many of us, many miles away from you, are thinking of you as you do.

So many forces are coming up to the surface from the bottom of things, life shaking at its core, exploding with the fierce intentionality of nature.I know many of you realize Hawaii is taking a hit for all of us.

Why Hawaii? I think because Hawaii can take it.

Unknown perhaps by the media and unnoticed perhaps by many, I have no doubt how many Hawaiians are treating this occasion with reverence, weaving around it an invisible, sacred container. Honoring the Mother, respecting her as she screams, feeling the deep and archetypal messages that erupt from the soul of humanity as they erupt from the center of the earth.

Beyond the level of material science, so many ancient powers are being summoned now: through dance, through song, through prayers, through ceremony, through individual and group meditations. I see the Islands of Hawaii surrounded by extraordinary powers both unleashed and summoned by the volcanic eruptions. And every soul either native to Hawaii, or called to Hawaii, is feeling the multi-dimensional forces at work as the earth transforms itself and humanity is carried up in its thrall.

Hawaii, they say, is the heart chakra of the earth. Hers is the heartbeat not only of earth's Mother but of all her children. She is speaking, and those with ears to hear are listening.

Dear Hawaiian brothers and sisters, those of you holding the space for the earth to do what the earth needs to do — through prayers and ritual and love — please know how many of us know that you are doing it for all of us. And we thank you.

We stand in attention and we bear witness, as you endure and navigate this stupendous hour. We know how much more is going on than is visible on our TV screens.

We salute you.
We pray for you.
We love you.
We are with you.
Carry us in your hearts with us,
as we are carrying you in ours.

May God walk with you.
May He bless you and protect you
And the earth on which you live.
Amen

xo
Marianne

May 22. 2018

Kekuhi Keli'ikanaka'ole is the Coordinator for the Center for Hawai'i Life Styles, UH Hilo. She's an award-winning singer, and a kumu hula, the eighth generation with Halau o Kekuhi, which bases its style of hula on the forces of Pele and her sister, Hi'iaka.

HPR's Noe Tanigawa reports, Keli'ikanaka'ole offers a different perspective on the current Kilauea eruption.

Kumu Hula Kekuhi Keli'ikanaka'ole says these days, the air is humid and warm.

Above, there are clouds that look like birds.

"You wake up in the morning with sulfur on your tongue.

It's enlivening in the body, very sensually, using all the senses."

Keli'ikanaka'ole says, aside from obvious disruptions, there may be a reason if people are feeling extra nervous or excitable.

Keli'ikanaka'ole: There's a quickening of energetics. There's another force that the Pele is very responsible for and that is the magnetic force of the earth. It's magnetic and we forget because we cannot see that force, all we can know is what's in our vision. But there's another force the Pele is very responsible for and that's the magnetic force of the earth. We feel that. Or I hope we feel that.

I would think we would, but nobody's talked about it. What do you mean by "the Pele"?

Keliʻikanakaʻole: I'm talking about the Pele as the element. Her primary form is lava, magma. And so when we think about the goddess, we don't think about an extra form outside of that. We see the form that we're seeing today on the news feeds or Facebook feeds. That's it! She's right there!

Keliʻikanakaʻole: It's creation right in the front of our faces. If we want to think of anything close to that, watch the birth of your child, watch the birth of your friend's child. I think that's the closest we can get to that form of Pele as a divinity. The goddess is an energy. The goddess is a resource.

On Monday, 5–21–18, lava was entering the sea at two locations, forming "laze" fumes, a hydrochloric acid mist caused by volcanic action on salt water. Here, the wind blows laze fumes along the shoreline toward the southwest.

Keliʻikanakaʻole: We know the island is still going to produce new land for a looooong time. That's why, reframe the way we're thinking about the activity that's happening right now, reframe it! It's not a destruction. It's a creation.

Keliʻikanakaʻole: We don't even know when this is going to happen again, and of course we grieve the loss of houses and things, but just re-frame our community's orientation to what it is that's really happening. Look! We're living right here and we're going to have stories to tell for the next one hundred years.

Keliʻikanakaʻole: Stories that we read in the Pele and Hiʻiaka books now, those are the things that were happening in front of people's eyes. So what do we do? Let's write it down, let's journal it, you guys. Everybody who has the opportunity to pick ash up from their windshield and go "Oh, my God," this was just made, and it just popped out of the earth not ten minutes ago. Write it down! Be the community geophysicist so that we have stories for our great grandchildren for the next 100 years. That's the benefit.

May 26. 2018

Barely slept and felt something
coming
Earthquakes and Explosion on
the daily
New Earth Ash in my mouth and
on my skin
We're becoming new humans
Something is happening within
What a primal existence
Each of us getting shaken
Each of us letting go
Tūtū is creating
This is life on a Volcano

May 28, 2018

Holy Ashes
Earthquakes wake me from morning dreams 5.0s
We guess the numbers and make it a game
Check out the newsfeed and see the Pele made
a lot of ground in Leilani
creating waterfalls and lakes of magma last night
And Halema'uma'u had an explosion this morning
The Wind is taking it to Puna and South
Ashes and Vog expected
It's Memorial Day
My feed is very biased
Most folks are like screw the US and its imperial regime
I don't disagree
And then some folks are honoring their family
members who passed in War
I briefly think of my own Ancestors and how
wars have altered our family's destinies
Wars of politics and love
I got peace on my mind
But the kind of peace that's domestic,
not outside of this bed even
My wife and I
We are navigating important choices

I leave the island in two days
I'm being sent to the Continent to bridge, learn, and write
Untangling, Rewiring, Exploring, Creating
As artists I know we will both unpack this and create
something beautiful
An alchemy of passion + medicine + madness + surrender
Love is a daily discovery and an infinitely insane journey
I'm suddenly ravenously hungry
She sleeps
I try to conjure up the energy to rise and make breakfast
But a magnetic pull of this earth and the Pele's got me glued
to this bed like an ancient obsidian
Grounded and locked in
The house continues to shake here and there
I feel that God Herself is picking up this home and waking us
up from our slumber
Wake up, Wake up, Wake up
Destinies await
Choose your own adventure
An island is birthing itself and so are you
Here's a tip, no choice is wrong
I remember a moment yesterday
We laid down on the grass soaking up the sun in the yard
I place grass on her stomach making shapes
She is deep in thought
I ask her, what are you thinking?
She says with innocence and clarity — what story I'm
willing to commit to and tell
As she proceeds to tell me Options A to G
I'm fascinated by the way she processes this existence

Which one is the most favored, I ask
Plan B. Laying here in the grass and going like this
(she makes grass angels with her arms and legs)
That memory, before getting out of bed, makes me turn to
her and embrace her
Because no matter what, Love is beneath everything
And these ashes, I want to gather them and anoint every
being I meet

Re-reading these notes and entries, I see the arc of my transformation just beginning. I was just considering separation in my marriage. I also see the contrast of the sensational apocalyptic depiction of these events that the world received through the media versus what the inhabitants of this island truly experienced. I see the visceral description I was attempting to describe then — the description of transformation and of the pain of death and the simultaneous crystal-clear awareness that we were birthing into new humans. We were covered in ashes. I remember feeling how as I ingested ashes every day and as they seeped into my skin and even into the garden, in the veggies we harvested and ate, somehow through osmosis, they were shifting our DNA.

These details were not being portrayed in the news. The news sensationalized the events. Perhaps because pain draws more views. The most reliable news we had was a local Hawaiian man who took it upon himself to start filming from his phone live on Facebook and reporting from Leilani Estates, the ground zero of the lava flow. His name is Ikaika Marzo. His reporting was full of heart. He was a Kanaka Maoli (Native Hawaiian) who knew Puna like the back of his hand. Sometimes you could tell while he was reporting how much his heart was breaking, too. Along with other Hawaiian families, he started Pu'uhonua of Puna (City of Refuge of Puna), which became a hub for displaced people and lava evacuees. The eruptions birthed leaders in our communities. Ikaika rose to his leadership by showing everyone his humble servant's heart.

When you're living through the earth igniting in fire and lava, it's an entirely different experience from within that the evening news doesn't even touch upon. The transformation — the deep lessons and epiphanies we become aware of during our personal apocalyptic moments in our lives — those are often not shown on the news. If they were, if it became normalized to explore and speak of our self-realization and transformation, if the reporters asked such poignant questions requiring deep inquiry, we would be ushering in heaven on earth really quick. We would be able to alter realities like climate change, like the increasing amount of freak weather conditions and calamities, like endless war, like mass shootings, like police brutality, like the reversing of basic human rights, like the corporate and political oppression of indigenous people … all the things that shock us and enrage us on the nightly news — if we explored them through the lens of transformation and gleaned the lessons from them instead of arguing about them and sensational-izing the pain — we would be in a different reality than we are in now. Healing and change would accelerate beyond our imagina-tions.

The saving grace here is our free will. Thank God. It is our birth-right to walk through the deaths, suffering, apocalyptic moments of our lives as awake and aware as we can muster. It is also our birthright to turn off the news and start telling more authentic stories, asking soul-penetrating questions within ourselves, our intimate relationships and our communities, and therefore trans-forming and birthing new realities from within. I've come to real-ize during these lava eruptions, that the earth will not wait for us humans to transform. It will crack, shake, erupt, corrode, deplete, burn and flood amplifying and mirroring the healing that needs to happen within us all. The deeper we can look within ourselves in these moments of massive global shifts, the more likely we will be able to learn the lessons we need to learn and heal the wounds we need to heal, so that our consciousness and actions actually begin to shift, and only then will things turn around on a global and ecological scale.

With a laser sharp focus of awareness and rawness like Anutosh exhibited in her last days alive, we can begin to live every moment of our lives with this level of sobriety. Death and destruction light fires under us instantly to drop our illusions just like that. Yet we don't need death, destruction or suffering to come to our doors to make the changes we need to within ourselves to live our most awakened, purposeful and passion-full lives. We can start doing that now, wherever we are on this planet. Whatever is happening around us, we have the sovereignty to light our own fires and with a sense of urgency, continue to heal and transform and start creating spaces and opportunities for us to heal, transform and create solutions for a thriving future.

In these pages, I will share with you a journey called The Luminary's Journey. It is a path of embodied awakening and service that was very much ignited by the volcanos I live between, the goddess Pelehonuamea and the wise and generous teachers along my path. The Luminary's Journey is our birthright as humans. To discover our divinity, our medicine, our magic and be able to share it with the world from inside out.

I remembered and experienced the potency of my light and gifts here on this island after a very dark phase of my life. I healed here. I continue to heal here. I transformed here. And I continue to transform here. I explored so many different versions of myself here. And She continues to rebirth me over and over again.

I compose this letter to you here at my desk in my healing retreat center between the dormant yet awakening volcano called Mauna

Loa and the most active volcano in the world called Kīlauea. It is so quiet right now besides the cacophony of different birds awakening and broadcasting their epiphanies of the moment. It's been raining for more than a week straight in this mountainous rainforest. The forest is growing fast, as the Jurassic hapu'u ferns unfurl themselves with so much audacity into their greatest expression. This is Pelehonuamea's country. The Goddess of the Volcano. Sometimes you will hear me refer to her as Tūtū Pele. Although I know she is timeless and multi-dimensional and not just a grandmother figure, I call her Tūtū Pele in reverence and as an acknowledgment of her ancient presence and medicine.

I know this is a divine appointment we've got here. You could be doing so many other things right now with your precious life, but you're here with me, about to embark upon a journey. I can feel you through the time machine as I write. You want to use your life and time on Earth as boldly and intentionally as you can. I get it. That's why you're picking up a book about creating a healing center and becoming a leader in this new paradigm we are ushering in. This will be my personal story of how I did just that. But more so it is a story of the Pele. Of what She taught me. It is very much about a place where life is primal and precious. Where the source of death and destruction is literally under our feet and remarkably and paradoxically, so is the source of creation, lush blooming life, and the New Earth birthing Herself on the daily.

At the moment of this letter, we are getting about four to five earthquakes a day here in Volcano. She, Pelehonuamea, along with all the other volcanic forces in this world infamously known as the Ring of Fire, are continuing to split the earth open every day. I check my Earthquake App as part of my morning ritual now, ever since last year with the eruptions, just to get a sense of where the portals are opening. How the earth is stretching and moving. I have an urgency to share this journey with you because of this knowingness that the earth is birthing Herself anew one earthquake at a time, and we, as her inhabitants and stewards are being awakened to create spaces of healing and transformation from the ashes of an Old World transforming Herself into a New. She will not wait for us to get it together. It is a miracle and privilege to be alive on this planet as She ascends at this time of the Great Shift. I know as she ascends, so do we. Just like a mother and the baby in her womb, we are deeply interconnected.

Marameng Salamat and Mahalo Nui Loa for taking this journey with me.

Darshan Mendoza
Volcano, Hawai'i
April 15, 2019

1: THE DARKEST NIGHT BEFORE THE DAWN

"Out of suffering have emerged the strongest souls; the most massive characters are seared with scars."
~ Khalil Gibran ~

I know it's about the last thing I ever want to hear when I'm *in it* — the clichés and platitudes of "focus on the light at the end of the tunnel" and "this too shall pass" and "what doesn't kill you will make you stronger." I always want to respond to that last one, "but what if *this does kill me?* Are you just going to sit there and watch my life end and then say, 'Oh, wow, it did kill her. Yikes.'"

If we do actually surface alive from these near-death experiences (physical but most often metaphysical) then these sayings are really 100 percent true and valid. But while we're *in it*, these are the most annoying things to hear from well-meaning loved ones. Note to self: stop saying it to others when they are *in it* too then. It's a habit I'm trying my best to break as well.

The spaces of darkness we sometimes find ourselves in, is similar to the Panic Rooms I've been seeing pop up in different cities I've recently been traveling to. It's a party game shop where people pay to be locked up and confined in a space they must escape out of. I remember seeing the first one in Chicago last summer. It stopped me in my tracks and I just stared at it for a while. The Panic Room (I think it was called). I read its poster advertisement pinned up on its glass door. And I thought, what in the fresh hell is this? It described different rooms you can pay to be locked in and the different scenarios you can possibly experience to challenge your escape. You have to figure out clues and crack codes and such. Sounded like a rush of fun, intriguing challenge and also a pending anxiety attack all balled up in one.

It got me thinking though, how we humans just love to project our feelings into curated experiences to ignite fear, panic, urgency, anger. When I was younger, I was all about pushing myself to edges artificially. And now, every moment of my life can organically elicit such feelings. I work with these feelings with a lot of my clients, I definitely don't need to create it artificially anymore. We've got the real deal happening in our everyday lives, in our own spaces within our consciousness, our own backyards and in the global arena.

Whatever your particular details are when you describe your dark nights of the soul, would you say that they have these themes:

1. You feel alone and unable to express your suffering to others?

2. You feel your mortality and the quickening of time and feel as if you've wasted your life away?

3. You don't feel seen, heard, validated, understood or loved?

4. You are overwhelmed by not only the state of your own life and the daily pressures you feel but the state of the world and what seems to be a quickening of its demise and annihilation?

5. You feel trapped and that there is no relief from this suffering in sight?

6. Life is changing so quickly (job loss, an ending of a relationship, a death of a loved one, you've become an environmental refugee) that you are paralyzed in shock, lack of control, and fear?

I'm sure you could list many more themes, but for the sake of not spiraling into a deep depression from just considering this list alone, I'll stop here. You get the gist. There are many reasons why we find ourselves in our panic rooms either in anxiety and stress trying to get out or curling up into the ball in the corner exhausted from trying. When you are *in it*, I suppose the immediate relief one can feel is to know you are not in it alone. There are people in the next room or perhaps even in the panic room with you, trying to crack the same codes and find the same clues so they can be free.

We've come to learn as we free ourselves over and over again from these dark nights of the soul is we wake up the next morning and the sun has not given up yet either and has risen again. Once we are free, we are left to be keepers of the clues and the codes. We get better and better at liberating ourselves. And because of that, our friends, family, colleagues, clients and even strangers are drawn to this sense of freedom we emanate. We've been through it and we in fact were not killed and yes, we are stronger, wiser, more humbled and more embodied than ever.

As I stood outside of that Panic Room from the bustling sidewalk of Chicago, I noticed the fresh escapees stumbling out from their doors. A multi-generational family it seemed. They were exhilarated, flushed in their cheeks, happy and laughing. Off to the next adventure — a beer perhaps and some pizza across the street.

How quickly one can go from panic room to pizza. It was surreal to me then because I just landed back in Chicago after leaving an island on fire and a people in the deepest transformations of their lives. I landed in a space so civilized and ordered, where artificially simulated Panic Rooms existed and took your money to scare the life out of you for an hour.

I see you as this traveler, like me. Walking around in a world that may not seem to match your inner world at all — your experiences and what you've been through. You have been on a lifelong pilgrimage in discovering the deepest meaning of your life and purpose. You are moving through the initiations and gauntlets laid out on your path like a spiritual warrior determined to crack this matrix. You may be weary. You've walked through some fires. You've escaped several panic rooms in your day. And you've got a heartful of codes and wisdom you are no longer willing to keep to yourself. I see you and most importantly I feel your heart's desire to walk this earth being a living, breathing testament of the light in these dark spaces you find yourself in. Because of what you have liberated yourself from, you are compelled to liberate and illuminate people and places you find yourself connecting with. I totally and utterly get it.

Know you are not alone despite how it may feel. Know you have just found a friend here, a co-creator and colleague. Aloha mai. And guess what? There is a tribe of Luminaries just like you, gathering together, resurrecting beautiful healing spaces all over the world, creating paradigm-shifting realities with their genius and light. We've all awakened from our panic rooms and sometimes, yes, we return to them only to realize we've already escaped them in the past and we have the codes within already. We have all acknowledged our calling and accepted it. We are embodying heaven on earth from inside out, from small victories to profound ones and all the unseen moments in between.

As the world undergoes the Great Shift that we are experiencing, old structures crumbling globally and in our own personal lives, it is integral that Luminaries find each other so we can co-create the realities and spaces that the earth, our Ancestors, Future Descendants, and God are asking us to. It can be a daunting task and at times overwhelming. The thoughts of: Who do I think I am to have this vision and create it? Who would come if I created this space? Where do I even begin?

1. Who are you to *not* be a vessel for this divine vision to come through? Who are you to *stop* this creation because of self-doubt?

2. Imagine all of the people trying to escape from their panic rooms. We are all healing and transforming as humanity. Who would come? Humans. Every kind of human on the journey of healing and transformation. They will find you. But you've got to rise up and let yourself be seen.

3. You've already begun. You read the first chapter. You're about to foundationally prepare yourself to answer the calling in your heart and share it with the world.

I'm hearing another question: *but what if I fail?*

What if you do?

The world will remain as is without your vision in it. Nothing lost, nothing gained. So why bother trying and risk failure? Why be born and come to Earth in the first place? Why play the game? Why liberate yourself and crack the codes?

One of my favorite hero's journey is *Into the Wild*, a story about a real-life pilgrim named Christopher McCandless written by Jon

Krakauer. If you haven't read it, do so or see the movie (Eddie Vedder's soundtrack is so epic in the movie too). I won't spoil it here for you with a synopsis but I will share one of the most impactful parts of the story for me. The author mentions that Christopher highlighted this paragraph from the book *Dr. Zhivago*:

> *"And so it turned out that only a life similar to the life of those around us, merging with it without a ripple, is genuine life, and that an unshared happiness is not happiness …*
> *And this was most vexing of all."*

Christopher scribbled a note next to this paragraph saying, "HAPPINESS ONLY REAL WHEN SHARED."

That truth sent chills down my spine.

Why bother trying? Because you've gotten this far already and perhaps the clue you have found recently is the fact that you have a vision to share with others and it will surely benefit some lives. That's why you will risk failing. That's why you will risk making a fool of yourself. That's why you will fail and get back up again many, many times. But more importantly, deep within you, you can taste the next code you're so close to activating within. You know that if you were to embark upon this endeavor bringing your vision to life, you will be transformed into the person that has the audacity to dare to succeed and put yourself out there for the benefit of other humans. *The gifts we came to earth with is only real when shared.* This is the next adventure calling you ahead. I suspect that's why you are here and that's why you've already taken the first step on your rise up. For a Luminary like yourself, staying complacent in the darkness is just not a viable option anymore during this Great Shift. Your light is just too bright to hide. The world and

Her inhabitants are calling you forth towards that dark birth canal. There is not just a light at the end of the tunnel, *you are the light* and there is *life* at the end of this tunnel, a *magnificent one* made up of all the gifts you bring with you to share with the village that awaits you.

2: HOLY ASHES

"In order to rise from its own ashes,
a Phoenix first must burn."
~ Octavia Butler ~

A Phoenix First Must Burn

My favorite smell in the world is lava after the rain. Upon landing at the Hilo Airport, there is this sweet, intoxicating smell in the air of sulfur being churned up by pelting rain on hardened lava. It is a forewarning to all those who land – whatever you have brought with you or whatever you may be escaping from will be unpacked, singed, and transformed upon arrival. That is the promise of this particular island. Its depth is up to you and how willing you are to surrender.

It is an elemental land. A land of extremes. It is the most isolated land mass in the world, surrounded by the Pacific Ocean. It is the home of the goddess Pelehonuamea and the most active volcano in the world. The cleanest air in the world has been tested and recorded to be at the eastern-most tip of the island in the District of Puna. You can throw an avocado pit on the ground here, without even burying it, and it will begin to sprout in a few days. That is the energy that surrounds us.

There are several mountain ranges here. Mauna a Wakea is the tallest mountain in the world from the ocean floor. There is a sacred lake named Lake Waiau nestled between its slopes, where Kanaka Maoli (Native Hawaiians) go to remember their lineage and source of connection, their ancestors and Father Sky and Mother Earth. Many children born on this land, have had the section of their umbilical cord, that eventually detaches within weeks of their birth, offered into the lake in ceremony as a physical remembrance to them for the rest of their lives of the Source they are connected to. The water is used for ceremony and sometimes to bless canoes. It is also brought down the mountain as an offering to drink to those who are sick, to bring vitality, and health. The movement to protect Mauna a Wakea, its resources and its sacred significance in Hawaiian rituals and prayers from further mismanagement, destruction and desecration is a movement that is currently igniting the World and showing everyone the power of aloha and the necessity to stand up for indigenous people's sovereignty and the natural resources for future generations.

Mauna Loa, meaning "long mountain," is one of five volcanos that make up Moku o Keawe (the Big Island). It is the largest volcano in both mass and volume. Its last eruption was March 24 to April 15, 1984. Prior to that 1950, and then one in 1926. Our retreat center is on the slopes of Mauna Loa. And across from the most recently active volcano in 2018, Kīlauea volcano. On the other side of Mauna Loa, on its slopes, is a high plateau called Pohakuloa. The US Military has occupied that area and regularly bombs it to train their soldiers defusing depleted Uranium into the air that often blows toward Waikaloa, where a majority of the hotels and resorts are on this island. Living on the other side of Pohakuloa, we sometimes feel our house shaking, the windows rattling, our ear drums vibrating, and our hearts breaking. Bombing the slopes of a dormant volcano seems like the most reckless decision I can't begin to understand. I have dreams of Mauna Loa erupting again. If She does, her lava is very fluid and will travel faster than Kīlauea's eruptions. It is a very energetic section of the island to live in. There are many artists, geologists and recluse visionaries that live in Volcano. We are the Fire Clan.

How I ended up on this island is still a mystery to me. Living in Hawai'i was never anything I ever dreamed of or even thought about prior to moving. There seemed to be a magnetic force that accelerated the deterioration of my life in Chicago and drew me to Puna, the land the goddess Pelehonuamea first arrived to with her family. Puna is in the south eastern district of the island where in 2018 the lava erupted from the ground and created rivers and waterfalls of new earth flowing into the sea.

I consider it a deep and sacred privilege to be welcomed to this island, allowed to stay, heal, transform, and learn from the wisdom of the people, spirit and land here. It is a humbling privilege to be a steward to these seven acres here in Volcano and to be a bridge for many to the land, people, ancestors and spirit of this moku. When I look back at the journey that got me here, it is nearly impossible to not prostrate myself on the grass and soil and cry tears of gratitude. If I didn't listen or if I didn't surrender to the forces bringing me here, I can't imagine how different my life would be.

Immigrant Blues and Taking the Red Pill in a Blue Pill World

I was born in Manila, Philippines, as an only child. I was named Beverly Jean Floro Mendoza. I was born into a huge extended family. The Floros and the Mendozas. Two different clans with lineages in architecture, art, farming, politics, law and business, and possibly a circus performer (my Chinese Great Grandmother Lola Mameng is a wild card and we are still discovering the secrets of her past to this day). If this is true, I like to imagine she was a magician or a tamer of tigers, a legacy I would be proud to own in my DNA.

Growing up in the Philippines amongst so many cousins and family members was a contrast to my life in America. Those first seven years formulated an ideal life. I remember on long weekends my entire family would travel to the province and visit the family farms. We'd fish, tend to the animals and fish ponds, prepare feasts – there was a lot of time to tell stories and enjoy each other's company. Those long weekends in the family farms are imprinted at the forefront of my memory and I've idealized it and continue to strive to re-create it in modern life now, in the retreat center here in Volcano.

We moved to Chicago in 1984 – the year the Chicago Bears made it to the Super Bowl. America was strange. Chicago in the 80s was very strange. We chose Chicago, because like most immigrants, we chose to be close to relatives. In this case, it was my Tito Ed and his family. Chicago in the 80s from my young adolescent eyes was a lot of big hair, tight basketball shorts, and keeping up with the Joneses (whoever they were). Racism felt like either everyone was the mean kid golden boy from *Karate Kid* or Daniel-san the underdog; there were obvious unfair disadvantages and privileges made very clear by the lines drawn on the sand and the rules of the game. The immigrant hustle was real. My mother worked three jobs and my father took on the night shift. TV raised me; I was a strange child who preferred Mr. Rogers, Donahue, and Oprah.

I also was a very observant child, and I figured out the rules of the game really fast, and I played it as best as I could. It was me and my parents against this strange new world which means as an immigrant you assimilate as best as you can, you work ten times as hard and maybe, just maybe you will get an invitation to sit at the table. Education was key to further your chances to get a seat at the table. Assimilation was the strategy. Don't shine too bright to receive too much attention because it can bring trouble, but at the same time do the very best that you can and beyond. It was a subtle nuanced and strategic dance between accomplishment and invisibility. It became the ingrained habits I have had to unravel since then. Some call it decolonization. Healing from and recovering from the oppressive dismissal of your humanness because of the historical and current trauma imposed upon your country, people and lineage by countries and people more politically, economically and militarily more powerful than you. In the spiritual language, it is a process of remembering your divine birthright and peeling off the social constructs that make you believe you are any less than divine.

I became a journalist and writer in my early twenties and continued to observe humans and this strange world from the safety behind my pen. Through my adolescent and young adult years, I could see now a budding medicine woman arising. As I mentioned

I loved to observe humanity and life. I also loved psychedelics – most especially psilocybin mushrooms.

These magic mushrooms became my greatest teacher in those years and opened up my consciousness to a different inner world. It let me peek behind the layers of this strange world that always perplexed me. I saw the connectivity of everything in relationship to myself. This armor that I was very comfortable hiding behind, safe in my observational deck, softened and often times disappeared. I was able to connect to people, nature, and myself in a safe place where I felt this omnipresent nurturing mother presence enveloping me and teaching me. I always felt so clear the next day after taking the medicine. Like my life made sense, like I made sense and the next steps in my life I needed to take made a lot of sense too.

Mushrooms were the first medicine and teacher I encountered that catapulted me into the realm of metaphysics and healing, unbeknownst to my experimental adventurous teenage self then. It was definitely ingesting the red pill in a blue pill popping world. In other words, what I had suspected all along, since we moved to America, was showing itself to be true during these psychedelic journeys. There is something deeper and more real in this strange new world, like a heavenly speakeasy was waiting to be discovered behind the façade of these concrete and steel buildings and strangers. We just had to pull off the layers.

A Heroine's Journey

Like Alice in Wonderland, once you commit to following the rabbit down the hole, you begin an adventure - a paradigm shift. Like Alice, my world turned upside down, beliefs and patterns unraveled, and I met the most unusual characters along the way: teachers and fellow pilgrims, sacred clowns and wise sages. I can remember exactly when the rabbit visited me. I was having a complete and utter nervous breakdown (now I call a breakthrough) in February 2005. Februarys in Chicago could be the most depressing time of the year in the Windy City. It's at the tail end of winter, where the only colors you've seen in months are white, grayish white, grayish black, and soot. It was the time of year when seasonal depression tends to affect everyone, even people with the sunniest of dispositions.

I was working as a journalist and editor in Oak Park and living in Pilsen. One morning I woke up and I just couldn't go to work, so I called off. I decided to stay in my apartment and all I wanted to do was lay down on the sofa and stare at the ceiling. I did that for seven days avoiding phone calls and visitors. I was deep in existential despair. Then something literally cracked. It felt like my insides were encased in a thin glass vase that suddenly just combusted and something inside me was released. My consciousness stayed with this "something inside me" and so I hovered above my own body on the sofa, bundled up under my comforter I dragged from the bedroom to my February Sofa Fort. As I hovered, I simply observed myself on the sofa and I also strangely heard her thoughts and was able to observe her feelings as if she was separate from me.

Just like those moments in cartoons, when the Roadrunner is running away from the Coyote and his consciousness catches up to his body and realizes he is running on air off of a cliff, only then does he drop. That's what happened to me. I was fascinated with myself on the sofa. Thinking, oh this poor child, and her worries. It's not *that* bad. She is just looping around the same racetrack and cannot see anything else around her. Mid-thought, I realized I was hovering above my body, close to the ceiling and the moment my consciousness realized what was happening, *boom* – I swiftly and instantly returned to my body.

"What was that?" was my first question. Followed by, "Who was observing me? If I was observing me, then who is being observed? Who am I now?" Good Lord. The rabbit had appeared taunting me to follow him. Because my mother is a psychic Scorpio, she called right in that moment. She asked how I was doing, and I could only muster, "I think I need to be checked into a place where I can stare at swans for a month. But not a hospital. I don't want to be drugged or anything; I just need some time to stare at swans."

After this confession and request, my family and I decided I needed to either take a leave of absence or quit my job. I was over-worked and needed to rest. I agreed, but I knew it was something much deeper than that. I was worried that I had created a life that I no longer wanted to live. I feared that I was stuck in an identity and role that I didn't want to be in anymore. I also felt like there was another life and way of existence, much more fulfilling then the one I was living, beckoning me to find it.

The script I seemed to feel trapped in was you graduate from school, you get a job, you climb to the highest position you can, you take vacations, you find hobbies, you drink and maybe do drugs to take the edge off on weekends and after work, you date, you try to find someone you can maybe live with and commit to love forever (?) and you have a family. This is the American Dream. This is what you worked so hard to find a seat at the table for. You're at the table, be grateful. Where was I when this script was sent out? I've come to realize since that February in Chicago, one of the deepest moments of despair for us humans, is not feeling aligned to the life we came to Earth to live. It's a kind of lost and loneliness that can really separate you from yourself, other people and this earth. The moment my soul longed for relief and a complete reset and redo, forces started to work behind the scenes that soon enough they brought me to Hawai'i.

Real, It Just Got

Before finding myself on Moku o Keawe (the Big Island), I was first brought to Waianae, the northernmost, westernmost part of O'ahu. It was also the most impoverished part of O'ahu. It was an immediate reality check on Hawai'i which like the rest of the world, I imagined it as nothing but paradise. The land was nourishing, the sea was vast, soul quenching and healing, the mountains were majestic and most especially the people – I've never met a more present, generous, funny and genuinely happy people in my life. I felt like I've landed home. All that was missing were my family. But I soon saw the strange paradox of this paradise. On the beaches from Nānākuli, Māʻili, to the stretch from Waianae to Mākaha – were tent villages where hundreds of homeless families, all mostly Hawaiian lived.

I lived with former high school friends who were teachers at Waianae High School and Mākaha Elementary. Some of their students lived in these tents with their families and when a note from school had to be delivered personally to their parents, there were no addresses to GPS, it was specific directions to what tent to find on what particular part of the beach. It opened my mind to the colonization of this land too. The same historical oppression and trauma the Philippines underwent under the Spanish, Japanese, and American occupations, Hawai'i was undergoing under an American Occupation, too. That is not in the history books at all about Hawai'i and certainly not in Elvis movies or the hotel brochures. I would have felt that reality check unless I lived in Waianae.

I was embraced by the community. I met a group of women who became my best friends to this day. Artists, Healers, Educators, Midwives, Activists – all wild women. We called ourselves the Urban Babaylans (meaning "priestess" in Visayan, a dialect in the Philippines). They are my sisters, aunties and mentors and we witness each other in our transformations and we meet often scheduling our gatherings around full moons, solstices and equinoxes like urban priestesses would.

Whenever anyone asks how I ended up on the Big Island, I say Pelehonuamea sent me an email. To this day, I have no idea how I magically received an email about Kundalini Yoga on the Big Island (a yoga no one in the world knew I just started reading about). It was the first of many, unexplainable divine interventions and bread crumbs left on my path. I took it with a plan to only stay for one month which turned into thirteen years and counting.

Unbeknownst to me, I had the beginning of a Kundalini Awakening in Chicago, during that dark night of the soul. Soon on the Big Island I was to meet my first teachers who would teach me how to embody this newly awakened life force buzzing inside my body with Kundalini Yoga and Meditation. It would accelerate my life, healing and transformation like no other. I lived in a tent on lava for one month during my training at a place called Yoga Oasis in Puna.

Sleeping on lava and doing Kundalini Yoga nine hours a day cellularly transformed me inside and out. I realized I was that consciousness. For the first time in my life, I felt really at home in my body. Subsequently my body started to get really toned and fit. I lost my extra weight I was carrying, my skin started to take on a glow, my eyes got very clear and my hair started to grow faster and thicker. I found just the right conditions for my soul and body to thrive. The more connected to Source I became, the more connected to my body I became too.

I had a newly ignited sexuality and fire within. I was constantly turned on about everything. The flower in someone's hair. The way a person's skin glistened after they got out of the ocean. The way the air felt around me. My heart just opened to feel in love with everyone and everything. I felt more authentically me or at the very least discovering who I really am in my core. Visions of different spaces and timelines I couldn't comprehend that seemed utopic and of another world, started to fill my headspace every day and night. I cried often in my tent as the movie of my life just played out at times while I laid there on the lava. I couldn't believe where I was one year after that winter day. I was grateful beyond belief. I was entering the rabbit hole full speed ahead.

Spirit kept aligning me to teachers and opportunities to fully immerse myself into Kundalini science and wisdom teachings, Filipino and Hawaiian healing practices, and what I call Jedi Super Powers. It was one immersion after the other followed by short rests of integration, but then back into the next teaching right away. I learned that I preferred immersions. I don't think I had a choice living on a volcano anyways. A fire was lit within me.

I learned early on how to discern the real teachers from the fake ones. And there were definitely some fake ones. By fake, I mean hypocritical, ungrounded, and sometimes even predatory in how they abused their power. I was also very suspicious of a kind of spirituality that was obsessed with ascension, get to the top of the pyramid and pay no attention to how you actually embody all of that wisdom and spirituality on Earth, with the people around you, with the actual soil you walk on, with your humanness. Today, I can see how patriarchal that kind of spirituality can be. I met a lot of teachers who didn't want to be in their humanness, who denounced it like a parent scolds a child. I was always suspicious of teachers like this. This discernment I call the indigenous discernment, rooted in my ancestors and my family. Perhaps it's the immigrant in me too, always side-eyeing American and Western everything.

Instead, I learned to trust my heart's wisdom and resonance. I learned to take the gems from such teachers, and leave the rest. I learned to flex my compassion toward teachers too as I recognized that they are also just trying to figure it all out – how to be human, how to heal from traumas, how to navigate pain, how to harmonize spirit, ego, mind, and emotions and this body of ours and our relationship to others and the world.

Despite these experiences with some false prophets and teachers, I was mostly blessed with incredibly embodied, humble and heart-centered teachers. My first teachers in Kundalini Yoga were both women, sisters, raised by a mother who was in the circus. In hindsight this gives me more reason to believe my great grandmother was part of a traveling circus. She must have guided me to these teachers with such a resonating circus lineage as like mine. I resonated with Guru Rattana and Guru Kirin, because they were sovereign in their teachings. Not dogmatic, very much embodying the Divine Feminine in the way they integrated, embodied and taught Kundalini Yoga and didn't bother with the hierarchical dogmatic rules. I loved that so much about them. My heart resonated with theirs.

I received my name Darshan from them. One day during a break from class, Guru Kirin saw me skipping across this bouncy floored yoga room and she wanted to call out to me but all she could say was "Darshan!" She couldn't remember that my name was Beverly. She approached me later on that day and she offered me this name and told me that she felt that perhaps God was giving me this gift through her and it was very odd that she couldn't remember my name all day. She asked if I was comfortable receiving it. I said yes with a very recognizable buzzing happening within my body. I've come to equate that as a resounding *yes!* when all my cells start vibrating. She surprised me with a name giving ceremony at the end of the day. Darshan, I learned, means vision of the divine. And divine sight. And also, a divine blessing. I was so deeply honored. Darshan. It's also gender neutral. Men and women have historically had this name.

I wasn't going to officially take the name on and start calling myself that. But two significant moments had me change my mind. One was this sudden memory that came up of learning what my legal birth name was. Beverly Jean. I was in first grade at St. Jerome Elementary in Chicago. And we were learning how to write in cursive. We began with our names. I started to write "Jinggay," over and over again. For all my seven years on Earth, that was the only name I ever heard people call me. My teacher walked by and looked over my shoulder to say, "oh that's not your name, dear." She took her roster out and points, and said, "This is your name. That must be your nickname. Your name is Beverly."

My first existential crisis at seven years old looked like this: I started to write "Beverly" in cursive, over and over again and held back tears. Who was Beverly? These letters are so unfamiliar. So, if you can imagine, being given a name in this ceremonial way healed a lot of that shock and disassociation I experienced as a child. When I told my mom about the name, she immediately loved it. I was surprised. It was her enthusiasm that encouraged me to take the leap and embody this name and vibration.

What sealed the deal of me taking on this name was meeting these two fascinating people who came into Perfect Harmony, a boutique in Hilo that I worked at. I considered this boutique a portal because the strangest things would always happen in this boutique. I met the most amazing humans there and received incredible messages there too. One day, the air conditioner placed above the door kept leaking. Occasional drops would hit people on the head as they walked in. I would acknowledge it by saying, "Oh, sorry about that, we'll be getting that fixed today. Consider it an anointing. Welcome and aloha!" No one found that funny. I stopped saying that after the first few times it bombed. This couple walked in later that afternoon right before we were closing. The woman got the water drip upon entering and she said, "Ah, an anointing!"

I said, "Yes! You're the only one that sees it like that, too!"

Immediately there was warmth and recognitions between us. She and her husband were such happy people, dressed in flowing white linen, relaxed and humble but their stature and energy was very big. She asked me what my name was and I said, "Beverly." She stopped and looked at her husband and they smiled at each other and she turned back toward me and said, "I'm sorry, dear, that's not your name. What's your real name?"

Surprised, I said, "Well, I was given a name, Darshan, but I haven't taken it or anything. It seems too big of a responsibility."

She laughed. And said, "dear, it's not about being prepared or waiting to be good enough to take on a name, it's letting the vibration of the name change you from inside out." She was so light in her confidence. She asked if she could see my palm and I showed it to her and she just held it gently and smiled and said, "Hello, Darshan, so good to meet you again." I was all kinds of buzzing within and just trying to keep it together at that point.

They dropped over a thousand dollars in those twenty minutes, buying pretty much all the buddhas in the store. They mentioned that they were invited over to Kauai that weekend by a small group of people to open up a portal so that the new Buddha, Maitreya, the Buddha of Joy can enter the planet. They suspect that he will be born somewhere in Louisiana. They were flying through the Big Island to connect to the energies here and then heading back home. They shared this agenda with me as nonchalantly as a tourist would share that they're going manta ray swimming at sunset. "Uh huh. Wow. Louisiana?" is all I could muster. They cheerfully took their buddhas and left. Interactions like this happened to me all of the time. The gift of staying open and curious is that messengers from God find you no matter what.

I was stunned and integrated that interaction the rest of the week, and soon after I decided to take on the name, Darshan. Ten years later, I learned from a Chinese woman I was attending Mystery School with in Joshua Tree, California that my name in Chinese meant "big mountain." *Dah shin,* she pronounced. She drew the letters for me. They looked like mountains. It was a homecoming for me in so many ways. I felt my Lola Mameng there in that moment. I saw her connect the dots. Chinese Circus Performer Badass Lola connects me to the daughters of a Badass Circus Performer Matriarch in America, I learn Kundalini Yoga and I receive a name, a couple from Florida tapped to help open a portal for the next Buddha of Joy to ascend on Earth, encourage me to take on the name and let it activate me, and then Lola Mameng weaves this conversation together with this Chinese woman and her ancestors at Mystery School, so that I can continue to embody the vibration of this name, a new layer upon divine sight, now big mountain. That's a very wild connect the dots but I'll take it. I've become accustomed with the unusual breadcrumbs the Universe loves to leave me usually dropped by the most unusual human angels on Earth. As Steve Jobs once said in a commencement speech:

"You can't connect the dots looking forward;
you can only connect them looking backward. So you have
to trust that the dots will somehow connect in your future.
You have to trust in something – your gut, destiny, life,
karma, whatever. This approach has never let me down,
and it has made all the difference in my life."

Perhaps the Chinese meaning of Dah shin was showing me that one day, I'll be living on the slopes of the longest volcano in the world. These breadcrumbs we collect along the way, in our journey, will show their significance one day. Even though you may not know how things connect, keep connecting the dots and following your resonance and heart, as you are a comet blazing your way through this constellation of life. Leave trails for others to see. Light paths for others to be inspired by.

For a decade, I learned and apprenticed under living elders and teachers from all corners of the world and many different traditions. I can see now what that accelerated course was preparing me for. I can see now why it was also so accelerated. I had a lot of catching up to do with my destiny as I spent a lot of my young adult days running away from it and assimilating into being "normal" rather than surrendering to and embody what was extraordinary within me.

The greatest teacher I met during this decade was Pelehonuamea. The goddess of the Volcano. I was able to hear her voice and interact with her in my dreams. I remembered how my dad is a dreamer. Ever since I was a child, he was able to dream about things that are happening soon in the future or somewhere else in the world simultaneously. Knowing I have a lineage of dreaming, helped me embrace this gift and I was always open and thrilled when the goddess entered my dreams.

You will hear more of these transformative initiations and teachings from Pelehonuamea I received throughout this book. Especially the initiations of embodment and the tests I received during the building of our healing retreat center here in Volcano. I was given plenty of opportunities to put these teachings into practice. I failed many tests, I licked many wounds, threw many tantrums (amusing the Ancestors) and got back up and tried again. Usually, the really important teachings and lessons needed to be imprinted through the process of trial and error.

I often refer to Tūtū Pele as your most fiercely compassionate teacher you could ever meet. The kind of teacher who brings you to the edge of all of your comfort zones, false beliefs, illusions, and fears. If you refuse to face them with her support, she'll just push you off of the edge of the cliff, knowing you needed that nudge and you'll be alright. As you plunge into the sea and find yourself crawling back to shore, she is the kind of teacher that is right there waiting for you, blanket in hand, ready to wrap you up in her embrace and walk you to the fire, warm you up and ask you what you've learned. I realize now that perhaps the warm, nurturing, motherly presence I felt as a teenager on psilocybin mushrooms was Her all along. She was the one whispering into my heart, "There is more to life than this." And She was the one calling me to the fire of my transformation, closer and closer until I finally took the leap. I'm so grateful I did.

After my Kundalini Rising Teacher Certification Program, I started practicing and teaching Kundalini Yoga all over the island. Teaching and practicing Kundalini Yoga three times a day was accelerating everything in my life. My karmic relationships, my embodiment, my awakening, my healing, my clarity. That is the time I started to see visions of the healing center so clearly. I was enthralled by the visions and simply started to take notes and document what I was seeing and learning. I had no idea how I could ever manifest these visions. I was teaching yoga for mostly papayas and art work students wanted to gift me. I was pretty convinced that I was leaving the world of money and stripping away societal structures more and more each day. But the visions were so strong and my surrender to this path of discovering who I am, kept me on the trail of this dream.

Spirit kept sending teachers and experiences my way in preparation to one day embody this dream and be ready to create it. It would be a decade long process. Mystery School, Healing Art

School, Bioenergetics Quantum Healing apprenticeship, epic love relationships, apprenticeships with several elders, healers, leaders and entrepreneurs and the wild messiness of being human on Earth ... all of it was my preparation. I had to burn down in layers. I had to rise up in layers, too.

Once you accept the visions and mission arising from within you, dear Luminary, if you haven't already experienced the quickening, your life will accelerate beyond your imagination. It will not kill you (although parts of the journey will entail many deaths of old identities and belief systems). It will awaken you. You will have divine protection and support. Because God wants this creation to manifest itself through you. You are the vessel for this particular light and frequency. It will ask everything from you - your surrender, trust and willingness - so that you can embody this level of love on Earth.

The smell of sulfur rising from lava after the rain – for the rest of my existence – will be the olfactory visceral memory I will always equate to transformation and embodiment. It perks me up and softens me at the same time. There is no scent like it in the world. It is the essence of this magnetic land of fire, transformation and creation.

3: THE LUMINARY'S JOURNEY

"I am part of a light, and it is the music. The Light fills my six senses: I see it, hear, feel, smell, touch, and think. Thinking of it means my sixth sense. Particles of Light are written note. O bolt of lightning can be an entire sonata. A thousand balls of lightening is a concert. For this concert I have created a Ball Lightning, which can be heard on the icy peaks of the Himalayas.
~ Nikola Tesla ~

Luminaries in Residence

Our healing retreat center in Volcano is rapidly evolving. We have created space for healing and transformation where we have hosted wisdom keepers from all over the world to share in their traditions and lineages with our community and the global guests we host. In the two years that we've been open (minus the seven months of being closed as the volcano was erupting) we've hosted the following retreats:

- Tandaan (to remember in Tagalog): an opening blessing and gathering inviting medicine men and women from the Philippines to share in their Ancestral traditions and modern ceremonies and practices.

- Vedic Fire Ceremony for Ancestral Healing: one of the oldest rituals in the world, a fire puja is a form of communication with the divine and used as a ceremony for healing, emotional purification, and transformation.

- Kundalini Yoga and Restoration Retreat: practiced sadhana and kundalini kriyas to restore our vitality during the winter while pampering ourselves with massages, spa and nourishing food.

- Tantric Love Coaching Retreat: a Kundalini Yoga perspective on love, intimacy and the balance of the Divine Feminine and Divine Masculine within each of us.

- Systemic Family Constellations, Business Constellation and Nature Constellation Retreats: these modalities were inspired by the Zulu Tribes in Africa and developed in Germany. The work uses this "systemic field" and "circle technology" to reveal unresolved traumas, disharmonies and misalignments in the family system, and other constellations like business, work and nature. It disentangles chords that can persist through time and space and become entanglements in subsequent and current generations. Once these conditions are acknowledged, a resolution can come to the surface that honors everyone and restores the flow of love and acceptance within the systems.

- Energy Kinesiology Workshop: an exploration of holistic health care through the art and science of muscle testing, where participants listened to the innate wisdom of the body to discover what's needed to create optimum health and performance.

- In the Midst of Healers: a gathering of indigenous, black, and people of color healers for rejuvenation, skill-share and storytelling building a web of interconnectedness across cultures from the Druid, Native American, Curandera, Inuit, Orisha, Hawaiian, and Filipino traditions.

We have also held monthly supper clubs, inviting chefs from all over the world to bring in their ancestral and innovative global fusion cuisine to our local community. The Filipino in me, I've realized, not only delights in creating feasts for our local community, but takes it on as my ancestral duty and mission.

In between these bigger gatherings, we host individuals on their healing and transformative journeys, creating personalized curated retreats using the many modalities we practice from cleansing and nourishing nutrition, bioenergetics quantum healing, integrated massage, acupuncture, ancestral healing ceremonies and ritual, Spiritual Release Therapy, Systemic Family Constellation work, sound healing and energy healing.

The lava eruptions of 2018 gave us seven months to cancel our upcoming retreats, rest and regroup. In that time, a new evolution and offering started to unfold. And that is called The Luminary Journey and Luminaries in Residence. According to Merriam-Webster, "luminary" means the following:

1: a person of prominence or brilliant achievement

2: a body that gives light especially one of the celestial bodies

After years of being primarily focused on hosting retreats centered around healing, transformation and Ancestral remembrance, a creative force started to arise on the land. And it made a lot of sense. The Volcanic eruptions sped up everyone's transformation – if you were still holding on to attachments that weren't for your highest good and divine alignment, Tūtū Pele and the lava cleared it away. People moved, people divorced, people switched careers, people had to heal sudden health concerns – it was as if someone pressed fast forward on the Space and Time Continuum Clock and it really didn't matter if you were ready or not. The eruption was also creating the newest earth in the world. One of the most magnificent embodiments of the Divine Feminine Force was pumping rivers of lava out into the sea. That is creativity manifest in form. So it was no surprise to me when I started to hear the guidance to create our new offering called Luminaries in Residence.

Luminaries in Residence is an in-house residency here at the retreat, for Luminaries like yourself, from all walks of life and traditions, who are holding within their hearts a vision they would like to manifest in the world. We holistically create a personalized and group experience where you are nourished, guided through healing and transformation and prepared to create your vision into reality. The guidance was for me to gather a tribe of incredible practitioners whose common denominator is their belief in and embodiment of magic. The magic part was integral because we will be using all of the tools of practical and quantum magic to prepare an individual to birth their idea into the world.

"So gather them," I was told. Gather the financial advisor (who happens to be quite clairvoyant), the web designer (who happens to be a heart healer and artist), the techie (who happens to be a qi gong teacher), the business coach (who happens to be a world-re-nowned psychic), the architect (who happens to also be a florist and wine maker). Are you seeing a theme here? Gather the heal-ers, the transformers, the spell breakers, the chefs, the teachers, the nature guides who are multi-dimensional magicians and who all believe that magic will transform the world. I realized upon these instructions that I'm being asked to recruit the Big Island version of the Hogwarts Faculty. What's fascinating about this mission is that I'm realizing I already know all of these magicians and it's been a delight to look at all of my colleagues, mentors, and friends and see their superpowers through these lenses. Making these calls and asking them to join us has been the most exciting to-dos on my calendar.

The Luminary's Journey is a curriculum of embodiment. Whether you are creating a healing center or an invention, work of art, a teaching, a business, a ministry or a movement, you are a Luminary the world has been waiting for. Through this time machine, our future descendants have been calling this curriculum and residency into existence, so we can help midwife you in birth-ing not only your vision but your divinity into an embodied reality.

Here is the Luminary's Journey:

L: Leave the Old Paradigm

U: Unpack Your Magic

M: Make Your Medicine

I: Illuminate the Shadow

N: Now Leap off the Cliff

A: Ascension Back to Earth

R: Root into Joy

Y: You Are the One You've Been Waiting For

The Divine Flow

This curriculum has been designed based upon the decade long journey I've personally been on in creating this healing center. There is an ebb and flow to creation. A process of multiple deaths, transformation and rebirths. It is also a dance between chaos and order, infinitely looping itself until you are ready to let your creation go out into the world. It is an intimate relationship between you and God/Goddess/Source/Spirit – whatever you call the Co-Creator of what we are experiencing. This Source is within you. As you continue to embody your spiritual journey, one lesson, initiation and milestone at a time, the manifestation of your vision will be more and more tangible. Your vision grows and embodies as you grow and embody.

There are moments where you will feel like you're hauling one brick up the mountain at a time to build your temple, falling plenty of times, and even tumbling down the mountain just when you think you've reached the summit. You will feel like giving up many times. These are moments that test your grit, stamina and faith. They will strengthen you and gift you with so much wisdom and embodiment. You will learn how to embrace these moments even if your first instinct is to run. Because often, these are where the most paradigm shifting lessons come from.

On the other end of the spectrum, sometimes you'll feel as if some kind of force is lifting you up and gracefully aligning all of the steps along the way and it is effortless. That's when you know you're in a zone. Ride that wave while it lasts. You'll learn how to see these waves coming, and how to align yourself to catch them when they come. How to elongate that ride too. Remember, there is a divine plan. There is a divine flow. And you are co-creating this with God. Your willingness to be all in helps you navigate this flow with a bit more grace and mojo. Either way though, the waves are coming, so pay attention and stay awake.

Consider this book a roadmap with marked booby traps and dead ends that may save you time and injury. You can choose to follow it or not. You can certainly take different routes and explore beyond the edges of what I've highlighted here. This is *your* Journey, and you are the only one that can truly uncover the way. Your heart will be the most accurate GPS. I encourage you to always follow that, but perhaps have this roadmap in your back pocket too. Just in case you may find yourself lost, frustrated, or alone. This is living proof that your dream is possible.

Healing the Vessel, Preparing the Womb

Before we dive into the creation process, there will be foundational preparations. The foundation is you. The foundation is your alignment and readiness. This is integral to prepare yourself for the conception, incubation and birthing journey of your idea. If you don't quite connect to the birthing analogy, consider the process of the earth and how trees grow. Before even planting the tree, one must prepare the soil. You'd have to weed and get rid of all the other roots hidden beneath the soil that will compete for nutrients and perhaps even suffocate the tree from growing any further. After the weeds are gone, you have to till the soil, level it out, and give it some air. And then you bring in some rocks, strengthening the soil for good irrigation, so that the water doesn't overwhelm the tree during heavy downpours. And then you find the proper mixture of nutrients, compost, manure, minerals and mulch so you can give this tree the chance to grow to its fullest potential by nourishing its roots and making sure they can root in deep. You have to undergo the healing, preparation and strengthening of your vessel before you even begin to draw the plans of your center/creation. This is the natural order of creation. Why reinvent the natural law? Let's recognize its genius and follow suit.

You May Be Birthing the Center but the Center is Rebirthing You

I often refer to the birthing of this healing center in Volcano as my own personal Mystery School. In the ancient times of places like Egypt, Mystery Schools were intense initiatory rites of passage schools where the initiates were taken from their homes and families at a certain age and entered into a strict and disciplined curriculum combining physical training and high-level esoteric arts and metaphysical training. The ancient Mystery Schools in Egypt sometimes had initiates jump into pools filled with alligators in the dark while blindfolded for extra measure. They were instructed to then find a narrow passage way in which they had to swim up to take their next breath of air. The consequence of not being able to use your intuition and instincts, hold your breath for an unlimited amount of time, and evade hungry alligators was not a D- in gym class, but death. Literal death. And yes, I compare co-creating this healing center to that. It often felt like life or death. It often felt unfair and too harsh. It challenged me on physical, emotional, mental, and most of all spiritual levels. And the lessons were not given to me in a neat little curriculum handout beforehand. It was often a surprise. And the teachers, they often came disguised until I started to smarten up and realized that everyone was my teacher, some I learned from positively and some I learned from negatively.

The greatest paradox and also the most potent blessing of birthing an idea into the world, is that this process of bringing it into reality will be rebirthing a new you. A more masterful and more tenderized you. A stronger and gentler you. Embodied Wholeness. The grit and the grace, that will be you. That's the gig. And if you have been tapped by the Divine and given the glorious blessing of being a temple creator, Earth steward, healer, teacher, heaven on earth bridger, innovating visionary, you best get prepared – as this is going to be one magnificent rebirthing.

The Orgasmic Birth

There are a lot of birthing analogies in this chapter, I know. But I couldn't think of a more profound act of creation in this Universe but the act of birthing another human being. I have a friend named Sayaka. She's had six children. When she was birthing her fourth, she was so relaxed and nonchalant about it she was texting me during her contractions in the comfort of her living room. Her midwife was about to arrive and she was getting ready to go into labor. I wished her a most amazing birth. I wasn't at all nervous for her, as she is such a Rockstar mama. And before saying goodbye, I wished her an "orgasmic birth." She texted me back right away and said, "what is that?" I briefly mentioned a YouTube video to look up of a woman being filmed by her husband having a legit orgasm during the birth of their child in a pool. Sayaka was intrigued. She said, she'll watch it right away. I lit a candle for her and the baby and awaited his arrival.

The next morning, I got a text from my friend saying, "Oh, my God, thank you for planting that thought in my mind, because I had a *big orgasm* during birth. He is beautiful." She called me the next day describing the moment in more detail and she said how Mike (her husband) was so shocked at what was happening, and got a bit embarrassed in front of the midwife and children when she was orgasmically birthing. She was enthused. "This makes so much sense to have an orgasm during birth. I mean, why not? This baby was conceived with an orgasm, why not be birthed with an orgasm!" she exclaimed. Excellent point. Maybe Sayaka had two more babies after that because of this phenomenon orgasmic birth thing, who knows. I was delighted with the gift the power of suggestion and her strong Rockstar mama belief gave her.

With that said, you can have an orgasmic birthing of your vision too. Remember the excitement, rush, and tingles when this vision first appeared to you? That divine energy unfolding within you can be sustained and amplified throughout your creation, even during the most challenging initiations, failures and obstacles. Some of the tools I learned in my journey that kept me going through my labor are these mind and heart hacks and grounded practices I've picked up along the way. I wish I knew of these from the beginning, it would have saved me a lot of suffering. That's why I'm devoting an entire chapter and section of the curriculum to it. It is integral to root your center and vision into joy, pleasure and the long multiple-orgasmic journey. Because joy is an incredible energy that is contagious and ripples far and wide. And the orgasm is life affirming and soul strengthening. As adrienne maree brown says, "You're not going to forget the suffering in the world just because you had a great orgasm. You're going to have more resilience for turning and facing that suffering if you're also in touch with the part of life that feels amazing, and not just the total catastrophes that are happening."

"so. have orgasms mkay?" she suggests.

Joy and pleasure are not only an incredible amplifier of energy but also an incredible magnetizer of energy. It's a win-win. Believe in an orgasmic birth, and you may be very happily surprised at the grace, synchronicity and vitality that is ignited in your creative journey.

Sovereign Divine Leadership

As we will continue to witness and be affected by the accelerating evolution of this spinning rock we are on, we will be called to continue to up-level the ways in which we show up for each other and ourselves. Our destinies. Our visions. Our creations. Imagine yourself when you've created this dream and it's actually this tangible space and these tangible experiences are happening within this space. Imagine yourself embodying all of the lessons along the way, all of the initiations and obstacles you've passed. You've become exactly what you set out to be and then some. When you're that aligned to God and a clearly grounded, rooted vessel for your divine expression, it will be a kind of joy and peace that cannot be described. Your humanness is in its most natural state when everything within you is working together in harmony and authentically interacting with everything external in your reality in harmony too.

This living tangible thing that you've bridged from a mere vision to a reality, it will need to be nurtured, protected, guided and loved to continue to grow into its highest manifestation. That's where you come in as the leader. Not just any kind of leader. A Sovereign Divine Leader. We will talk about what that means more in the chapters ahead. But in a nutshell, this kind of leader is on the new paradigm level. A leader who is self-realized. A true servant in ushering in heaven on earth through her own embodiment.

She is willing to be seen in her vulnerability and authentic human self. Someone who is owning all of it. Aware of her shadows, and using her light to illuminate them within, so she can radiate her wholeness from inside out. That's the embodied Luminary. That natural state of being is the destination of our journey we are about to embark upon together.

4: LEAVE THE OLD PARADIGM

"It is the worst of times because it feels as though the very earth is being stolen from us, by us: the land and air poisoned, the water polluted, the animals disappeared, humans degraded and misguided. War is everywhere. It is the best of times because we have entered a period, if we can bring ourselves to pay attention, of great clarity as to cause and effect. A Blessing when we consider how much suffering human beings have endured, in previous millennia, without a clue to its cause. Gods and Goddesses were no doubt created to fill this gap. Because we can now see into every crevice of the globe and because we are free to explore previously unexplored crevices in our own hearts and minds, it is inevitable that everything we have needed to comprehend in order to survive, everything we have needed to understand in the most basic of ways, will be illuminated now. We have only to open our eyes, and awaken to our predicament. We see that we are, alas, a huge part of our problem. However: We live in a time of global enlightenment. This alone should make us shout for joy."

~ Alice Walker ~

Phasing Out of the Old Paradigm and Birthing Ourselves into the New

The Journey of the Luminary begins with leaving the ordinary and familiar world. Not to never return, but with the intention to return with more self-awareness by embracing both the light and the dark within oneself. When the Luminary has reached this wholeness, she is ready to return to the world to share the wisdom and medicine she has cultivated from deep within her embodiment.

Can you believe that we specifically chose to come to Earth at this exact time for this exact Shift of the Ages? Could you imagine that we vied for this opportunity? And that amongst the legions of other souls and beings in this Multi-Verse, we, humans, are the over-achievers, the super rebellious and radical souls, that not only volunteered but *campaigned* for a spot in this Earth School? This exact time in the time and space continuum we find ourselves in is what our souls have been preparing for in all of our multi-dimensional lives. This Great Shift, as the Sages have called it. Where internally, our consciousness is making a great leap out of the shadows into an awakened awareness and therefore, externally, the world at large is also making this incredible quantum leap as well. Quantum leaps are often preceded by chaos. We are in the midst of an accelerating chaotic time, in our personal lives and in the global stage.

This metamorphosis can be the most chaotic string of events in your life and can be quite destabilizing. It takes the most radical honesty and commitment to being human on Earth and discovering what that all means. It means that when this Great Shift continues to accelerate, we are centered in our humanity and spiritual embodiment so that we can actually anchor in and birth new realities and frequencies from within ourselves. This centering and grounding into our humanness through spiritual embodiment is a curriculum of all curriculums.

For this reason, I bow down to you right now, dear Luminary. As we begin this journey together, I'd like to anoint your feet because I recognize what you have walked through just to be here now. You have traversed up the mountain and you have decided to come back down to share what you have learned. The destruction, the fires, the storms, the earthquakes and the eruptions — your beingness tell the stories of your transformation.

My promise to you is I will take every chance I get to take you to the edges of this journey and ask you if you're ready to leap again, over and over and over again and I won't hold back the truth about the obstacles and challenges coming your way nor will I hold back the magical tools either. And I will only see your success with each step and giant leap. Where am I asking you to leap? Deeper and deeper into your wholeness as a human embodying God within your cells. Why? Because this is how we are going to manifest what you envision in creating and offering the world. You are going to create this as an embodied spiritual human being. It's going to take that kind of wholeness and integration for anything created to last and be solid in the New Earth.

The Luminary's Journey begins here at this basecamp. Here, we will make sure that the old ways of being and thinking have been digested, processed and released. We are checking your luggage, so to speak, before we traverse any further. What are you still carrying that will not only be of no use to you, but it may even weigh you down and sabotage your journey of embodiment? This is a crucial step in creating anything and embarking upon a new endeavor, especially a healing center. Because at the most inopportune (yet divinely aligned time of course), these old paradigm belief systems and ways of being we carry will bring things to a halt, so we can have another opportunity to authentically digest it, relearn the lessons and realign ourselves to our wholeness once again.

So don't underestimate or skip this step. It is common for us to think, well, I'll never have to learn *that* lesson again. The moment that thought even enters our mind, we've already tempted the fate dragons and something behind the Wizard's curtain is surely brewing to test us in our wholeness. Can you embrace this? And this? And this? Can you love this? How about that? And that over there? That's basically what happens as we take this journey down the mountain and embody our divinity. The old paradigm is one of duality. Of saying, I will help you but *not you*. I will love this but *not that*. It's a Paradigm of Fear. We cannot resist anything in the new paradigm.

If you reject any part of yourself, you are not whole. And if you reject any part of reality, especially your emotions and the healing you must do, you are not whole. And from my experience, Life will keep repeating itself with the same tests until you embrace it all and love every single aspect of your experience, and your embodiment. From that place a new paradigm can be born. Where humans are so embodied in their humanness that there is no duality between Spirit and Material, between Spirituality and Humanity.

The Fatigue Failure of Metals

Buckminster Fuller is famously quoted for saying, "You never change things by fighting the existing reality. To change something, build a new model that makes the existing model obsolete." For us to create new models that are meant to improve and evolve our experiences on Earth to entirely new levels, we must be well versed in the old models and in understanding how they worked and most especially how they *don't* work and why they were susceptible to break down.

Like structural engineers assessing metal structures and their strength and longevity, we can explore different areas in our personal lives and also in the global sphere and see where microscopic cracks may be forming — especially if we are willing to put a spotlight in these areas. The key word is *willing*. As Luminaries, if our deepest prayer is to be vessels for divine work and expression, then this willingness to look for cracks is a prerequisite to embodying this prayer. It is creating a true foundation of integrity within ourselves and what we create. This level of vulnerability and self-examination for a Luminary, is the kind of radical transformation we are all capable of and being asked to embody.

So let's shine the spotlight. As Marianne Williamson says, "The laws of consciousness apply to everything. Anything, when truly seen for what it is and surrendered to the higher mind, begins to self-correct. But what is not looked at is doomed to eternal re-enactment, for an individual or for a nation."

On Love Relationships

I find intimate romantic partnerships to be the most mind-boggling, earth shattering, bring-you-to-your-knees subject. As Elizabeth Gilbert once recalled in *Eat, Pray, Love* — she has traveled the world talking to folks about everything and anything, and the common denominator of all conversations, ultimately is the subject of the heart. Yogi Bhajan, the Kundalini Yoga and Meditation teacher who brought this yoga to the West, had always told his students that if you wanted to practice the most challenging and transformative form of yoga, be in an intimate, love relationship. This is why we shall begin here. It is an incredible catalyst of transformation in our lives. It can support and amplify our life work in the world and it is the closest to our hearts along with our soul missions. If you haven't yet noticed, we are working from the inside out here — so we might as well start at the epicenter of our individual Universes — the heart, through the quantum leap called love.

Marianne Williamson asks, "Can the purpose of a relationship be to trigger our wounds?" What an innocent question. This simple, piercing question can open up our Pandora's Box.

Marianne answers:

"In a way, yes, because that is how healing happens; darkness must be exposed before it can be transformed. The purpose of an intimate relationship is not that it be a place where we can hide from our weaknesses, but rather where we can safely let them go. It takes strength of character to truly delve into the mystery of an intimate relationship, because it takes the strength to endure a kind of psychic surgery, an emotional and psychological and even spiritual initiation into the Higher Self. Only then can we know an enchantment that lasts."

Let's take a nice deep breath here, and perhaps read her answer a few times over. There is nothing much more I can really say here but to stress the importance of investigating for ourselves the shadows and wounds unearthed to be healed from our intimate love relationships past and present. The easiest way to compile this list is to think of the ways our ex-partners or current partners continue to trigger us.

I write this from a place of being newly divorced. In fact, the judge has yet to sign the divorce decree as I write. So I don't consider myself a relationships expert whatsoever. I am, however, well versed and newly rebirthed raw and real from an epic marriage of two passionate artists and an equally passionate divorce where I've spent countless hours asking myself these same questions. Where am I still triggered? Where am I still resistant? What is left to be reconciled? What patterns are left to be healed? These are my wounds. And therefore opportunities to shine light, to embrace and to make myself whole again.

For me, my wound is being lied to. My wound is emotional and physical abuse. What can I embrace? My wounds that allow myself to be lied to and the ways I lie to myself. My wounds of self-worth and betrayal manifesting themselves through self-sacrifice, rescuing, and control. What are the shadows that these bring up? My pent up anger. How can I express anger in a healthy and effective way? How can I communicate boundaries without a charge allowing space for transformation in my delivery? How do I ask for support and help? These are huge opportunities for healing and radical honesty with myself. Relationships are the deepest psychic surgeries I have yet to find in this human experience. I continue to do the work within. It's liberating work. It's deeply vulnerable work. And it translates through everything in our lives. Most especially in how we show up for ourselves, our visions, our life work and our communities.

Ultimately, as we evolve as a species so does our consciousness around love, marriage, partnership and intimacy. We are continuing to discover how much more capacity we have in embodying whole authentic love within ourselves and toward our chosen partners as we realize what accelerators intimate relationships are to our self-realization and embodiments. As a generation, I am finding that we are unlearning the old paradigm programs on love relationships. We are awakening to the realization that as individuals we do not need to come together in some kind of co-dependent union to complete one another, hide behind one another or make one another happy. Doing so is a disaster and impedes our growth and sovereign embodiments tremendously.

As a generation, new understandings are arising from the old. As we continue to understand that we are spiritual beings living a human experience, the initiations, challenges, opened wounds, and healing within relationships are held with a devotional commitment that no matter what, as individuals we will use these opportunities to evolve, grow, transform and heal. Intimate relationships, when held in this level of awareness have an unbreakable purpose. It is probably the most accelerated rocket ride to self-realization especially if you're holding it as such. And it becomes a gift to the world.

With that said, it can be excruciating to stay in relationships with partners who are not willing to look within themselves to heal, transform, and grow. When both people are not devoted to self-responsibility and growth, a union can falter and break. Sometimes, the greatest gift lovers can give one another, is the gift of letting go and releasing one another so that both individuals have the better chance of realigning to their highest alignment and evolution. What I have learned this year as my marriage dissolved, is that if you can release one another while keeping your heart open (clear boundaries of course, but being absolutely present to everything that is unearthed in the process), it is an incredible opportunity for the deepest healing and transformation possible. The key is the open heart. And it is the hardest to do. It's counterintuitive to self-preservation. The secret is to embrace every piece that shatters. It can be so much more painful but I am realizing it is *the* gift of love. It will transform us and bring us closer than we've have ever been to our divinity.

Find your mentors in this journey of love. We've got friends who are modeling sacred unions and also friends who bravely and vulnerably embody conscious uncoupling. My models and relationship goals are Jada and Will Smith. While I was going through my separation, I watched Jada's *Red Table Talk* with Will Smith as they dissected and vulnerably shared the lessons of their marriage, the break of their marriage, and their newfound partnerships. It reflected to me everything I was learning from my marriage. It showed me how we cannot make one another happy, it showed me the importance of showing up whole and full in a relationship so you don't deplete one another, it showed me the importance of clear guidelines in communication, it showed me the power of the willingness to end the old structures of marriage if it doesn't serve the love, and it showed me the importance of creating partnerships founded on sovereignty, wholeness, and unconditional friendship.

I dedicate this next decade of my life to this kind of devoted love. And the foundation of this is a fully embodied and devoted me. So I can show up whole. I can show up full of joy and pleasure. When I look back on my relationships with this deeper understanding, I break out into my own rendition of "To All the Men and Women I've Loved Before." I send them quantum notes of gratitude for what they illuminated within me and of how they softened my heart and expanded its capacity to experience love in this life.

Know that when you accept your divine mission, dear Luminary, every aspect of your life becomes illuminated and your intimate romantic partnerships are one of the most foundational aspects of your life that will be examined. It will either support your divine mission through transformation, healing and inspiration (with deeply transformative work by you and your partner) or it can take a lot of your energy and time away derailing you from your path if both parties are not willing to do the necessary transformative work. Be ready and willing to shine the light in those areas and make decisions that will keep you aligned to your journey of sovereign and joyful embodiment of your spiritual gifts in this wild human life. And remember that an open heart and willingness to be present to all that arises is the key.

On Health

When physical sickness and disease begins to manifest, it is the last-ditch effort of our soul telling us that something has been out of balance for a while. Even a common cold is a red flag that for some time now our immunity has been compromised and has been fighting off bacteria and pathogens to a point of exhaustion. Even a sprained ankle, which seems so random at times, is also a red-flag-waving moment from your Higher Self to get your attention. Ankle sprains are often connected to the fear and hesitancy to make a change, to leave a situation or relationship, to pivot a business, etc. There is often the emotion of guilt and fear involved.

Physical sickness are the manifestations of spiritual, mental and emotional disharmony also often combined with external physical pathogens. The physical ailments of the body are often the last sign of disharmony. Depending on the severity of the physical, mental, emotional disharmony, it will give you pause to consider the way you will heal and come back to balance. Allow the pause. Embrace it, even. As the saying goes, "What you resist, persists." Take this moment as an opportunity to learn more about yourself and what harmony feels like to you and the signs of disharmony. This is an opportunity for self-discovery through this disease and sickness.

For healers, this is often known as the first initiation, where Spirit challenges you to shift your perspective, ways of living, eating, breathing, moving, thinking, expressing and feeling to bring harmony and authenticity in the embodiment of your divine nature. As Anita Moorjani writes in her book *Dying to Be Me*, where she died, had a conversation with God, and came back to life to share this message of embodying our authentic selves: "Cancer is just a word that creates fear. Forget about that word, and let's just focus on balancing your body. All illnesses are just symptoms of imbalance. No illness can remain when your entire system is in balance."

In my practice of bioenergetics medicine, I've witnessed thousands of ailments in their pre-physically manifested forms, when they are merely just in the electromagnetic field of the client. Perhaps they are an energetic resonance connected to a worry, stress or belief a client has. I've experienced over and over again with each session, how once we acknowledge the possibility of this physical manifestation and bring it to our awareness, pinpoint its resonating emotion or belief, its biofeedback resonance weakens and often disappears. It's literally a quantum psychic surgery. I've witnessed physical disease already made themselves known in the body and mind to the client's primary physicians and doctors, also quickly bring themselves into harmony by acknowledging and healing their mental, emotional, and spiritual resonance. Of course, addressing the chemical and physiological imbalance is just as important, but as we have come to evolve to realize, we must treat the whole human being, as all parts work together and are connected to one another.

Consider this particular breakdown in health (from the most minor to the most life threatening) as an incredible opportunity for you to discover the next level of balance and harmony within yourself and with this earth and the communities, organizations and interpersonal relationships you exist in. From the microbe to our cellular structures to the roots of trees beneath our feet and to our families and communities we interact with, our interconnectedness is so profound and is the intended divine genius of our design. We've only cracked the surface and science is beginning to catch up to what the Sages have been saying since the ancient times, we are one and there is a cure for every single disease known to mankind. It is within us and it grows from this earth, it is in the elements and the genius design of nature, we just have to bring it to our awareness and pay keen attention.

An old paradigm way of dealing with health is to simply treat the symptom. To cut, and have surgery, or to numb and repress with medication. And then send the patient off as healed as long as the symptoms have subsided. The new paradigm is treating holistically the whole human being and the emotional, mental, spiritual roots that connect to the physical. Our physical bodies are designed to function at its optimal levels and to always bring themselves back to harmony and balance in the right conditions. Rest, laughter, delicious, and nutritious fresh food, sunlight, salt water, sweating, movement, dance, joy, deep breathing, love making create the right conditions. Allowing the disharmonic feelings of fear, anger, stress, anxiety, environmental toxins and bacteria to ripple through, cleanse it through — just as fluid as joy and water — so they do not get stored within our cells is just as important too. Embracing it all tells our body to stay fluid, loose, light, and moving toward alignment and harmony all of the time. It holds on to nothing and it also embraces everything, trusting in its divine intelligence to balance, cleanse, realign as it should.

On Careers, Jobs, and Money

After relationships and then health issues, I would say that careers, life purpose and money are the third biggest issues clients ask me to explore with them. Why am I here on Earth? How can I live a more purposeful and fulfilling life? How can I get paid in doing what I love? Often these questions are ignited because they are losing their jobs, or their work environment has become so toxic they are beginning to get physically ill or extremely depressed and unmotivated or they are constantly worried about money. It is our human nature to avoid change to the point that the Universe has to take away something we are clinging to in our comfort zones out of our fear to change. Beneath this fear of change, when explored deeply, is this fear of our true nature, gifts, and power. There is an incredible responsibility when we have fully acknowledged our gifts. It's a responsibility to hone it, protect it, grow with it, and then eventually share it with others and expose ourselves to be seen and to be vessels of it for others. It is absolutely vulnerable and scary. There-fore, we have gotten so good at creating excuses and hiding behind excuses so that we don't have to use our super powers. We don't have to be fully embodied. We do love our exit strategies, don't we?

If you need the motivation to leave your job or career that no longer aligns to your values and embodiment, look for examples around you of people making such bold leaps. Learn from their process, the way they phase out gracefully and in the pace that is best for them. Observe the work they are willing to put in to make this transition work. Observe their happiness and glow in their new alignments and use that as a motivation to make that leap yourself.

Start to explore what truly interests you. Start to explore week-end workshops, retreats, or even school programs that will get you aligned to what inspires. Being part of a community of like-minded souls is key to making your transition supported and graceful, so it won't feel as if you're pushing off into the abyss alone. Slowly make that shift from your job that no longer inspires you to a ser-vice, project or career that does. Rest assured that if you continue to stay in a job that makes you miserable and even sick, soon the Universe will conspire to get you fired or worse, unable to show up for your duties, in the form of physical sickness. It's just how the cookie tends to crumble. Don't take it personally even though it can feel *so very* personal. As in most crumbling situations in life, if you can find a way to embrace it and see it as a gift, a more divine alignment will come quicker for you to take. These are one of those codes I have discovered in this journey. It sucks that it's like this, but how else can God get through to us when we're in a deep denial or stagnancy about our divinity? Don't miss that opportunity. If we wallow for too long in the loss, we will miss the signs along the way pointing us to our next destined alignment.

Stay awake through this paradigm shattering change, and keep dreaming big about all of your deepest desires and visions, because God is most definitely listening and tuning in to what you are broadcasting at this very vulnerable, raw and surrendered state of your existence. Your broadcast is very clear at this moment. As it usually is during our "dark nights of the soul" and crossroads of our lives. So even if you're shaking in your boots and worried about how you will pay for your mortgage or perhaps even your next round of bills, stay focused on what you are asking for in support and alignment and what brings you the most joy. You are a potent magician at this time, in your most vulnerable, stripped, and surrendered.

Make sure this is *your* dream. Don't succumb to the old habit of conforming to what others want you to do either. There will be a lot of advice coming your way, especially if you reveal this career change. As Oprah Winfrey writes, "Often we don't even realize who we're meant to be because we're so busy trying to live out someone else's ideas. But other people and their opinions hold no power in defining our destiny." This is a time to become very intimate with yourself. What wants to be expressed through you? How? Where? With/for whom? These are questions only you can answer for yourself. Write these answers down. Treat it as a sacred ritual in which you are invoking magic. Because you are. Be intentional as your slate has been wiped clean. While you're at it, if it's resonant to you, write a thank-you card to your boss/job for the lessons and experience you gained and that will amplify your broadcast even more for what you're invoking next in your journey.

On Family

Clarissa Pinkola Estes writes, "Do not cringe and make yourself small if you are called the black sheep, the maverick, the lone wolf. Those with slow seeing say that a nonconformist is a blight on society. But it has been proven over the centuries, that being different means standing at the edge, that one is practically guaranteed to make an original contribution, a useful and stunning contribution to her culture."

Our families — ancestors, grandparents, parents, children, siblings, aunties, uncles, adopted families, chosen non-biological families … the whole shebang are the soulmates we have chosen to incarnate with, interact with and learn from in this Earth School. In fact, you've scripted the whole thing. What roles you will play. The dynamic (often dysfunctional) you scripted all of this together. Then you took a pill to create some kind of amnesia effect so that you don't remember that you produced, directed and wrote this entire experience. And then you all begin the play and then we spend the majority of our lives untangling these relationships and healing from them. That is the role of family, just like our intimate romantic partners. The thing with family is we think we don't have a choice. But we actually consciously chose them too before coming into this incarnation.

I've had relationships with people and have had clients who have had unfathomable abuse from their families. It is very difficult to navigate the healing from such abuse, abandonment, and trauma and to see it as somehow chosen and scripted by our souls before even entering this Earth School. In my healing work with people, I have found that in perceiving the dynamics and our family members (especially those that have caused pain and trauma) as part of the soul group we chose to learn from, it gives a much more focused and concentrated force of energy toward healing and finding the medicine from each experience.

Returning the responsibilities that are not ours back to our family members was a pivotal breakthrough I received through Family Constellation Work too. Where each family member takes back their roles, their destiny, their karma and the family system realigns itself in the proper order and relationship amongst each other. An example of this is often times, for Luminaries there comes a time in their childhood where they become the "responsible one" and the parent in family dynamics. Often it is the healer/black sheep in the family that is given the divine mission to disrupt the inherited and unexamined programs, illuminate it, and transcend it. These roles can make the Luminary into a scape goat and often the Luminary can take on a lot of projections and therefore pain and wounding. As the Luminary moves into adulthood, into her path of service, into other communities and relationships, these wounds are illuminated to heal and often we can root them back to these family dynamics and old roles. Systemic Family Constellation work can quickly highlight where the misalignment was, or when the roles became fixed and unravel them and realign them to much healthier formations. This is important work for Luminaries to undergo as it can liberate us from family patterns, dynamics, and destinies that can sabotage how we show up in the world.

Our family members are our greatest teachers and reflections. For our biological family members, we share the same DNA. And as epigenetics has proven, we are healing and experiencing the same experiences, fears, and trauma as our ancestors. This is all for our evolution as a soul group/family and on the macro scale — as a human species. Often, our most potent medicine and gifts are developed within the healing we need to undergo because of our family dynamics. This is your laboratory. And it begins in utero.

If you find yourself to be the black sheep in your family, you are in incredible company. Most Luminaries often are the odd ones out. You came with a different mission and often a slightly different, if not completely different frequency. You may have even been immune to that amnesia pill and remember more than anyone else in your family. This often makes it a very difficult childhood as you recalibrate yourself to earth and these dynamics. If you're lucky you found people along the way (if they are not your family members) who recognize your gift and uniqueness and they reflect to you your gifts. People who can really see you. Nevertheless, you know it now and you can begin to (if not already have) fully accept your mission to anchor in healing, awakening, forgiveness, compassion, transformation, truth, love into your family and into this world — and you often have to experience the opposite to create this kind of awareness and medicine to share and embody.

On Death

For most of us, the older we get the more experience with death we have. We are also more aware of our mortality in this Earth Walk and see time and space with more limitations usually. When we have our own brushes with death and experience our mortality either through a near death experience, or illness or sudden loss of loved ones too young, we value life so much more. We cherish the moments we have on Earth; we pay attention more to our breath and the influence and relationships we are having on those around us. It's a sudden reprioritizing of what's important in our lives. These are the gifts death brings us. This is often heightened after death visits and then it starts to ware off as we slip back into our normal routines again.

I've been paying close attention to Thich Nhat Hanh lately. Currently, he has returned to Vietnam, and consciously living his last years in preparation of his transition. He has been talking often of death and is using this opportunity to continue to enlighten us on this mysterious and profound aspect of life. He has been quoted in saying, "We should live every day like people who have just been rescued from the moon." I often play this game with myself too, when I'm feeling "bored" with life or fall into a monotony. Although, it's been a while since I've been "bored" — but I remember when I was in my twenties filled with energy, possibility, visions and stuck in a nine-to-five job post college, I would "pretend" that I've just arrived on Earth from another planet. I perceived things with awe and curiosity, shifting my jaded and "bored" perspective as a twenty year old. Now in my forties, it is the presence of death that lights this fire within myself to live life as presently, awake and fully as I can. I often hear my spiritual mentor, Deborah Jones, of Nine Gates Mystery School, saying in her Louisiana accent, "sta-aaaaay awake," reminding me to not sleep during situations I normally would default to by checking out. Let's stay awake and let death be our greatest teacher of savoring the nectar of presence and awareness.

When our loved ones pass, this too can be quite a paradigm shifting moment. Our hearts break, we miss them terribly and our world and experience of the world automatically shifts without their physical presence in our lives. When it's a violent and senseless death, or a death chosen through suicide, it can unearth deep intergenerational pain for the entire family and community to heal. In the shift of the new paradigm of perceiving and living, we are realizing more and more as a species, how death is a mere shift in dimension/change of address, transference of energy and form. We heighten and deepen our ability to stay connected to our loved ones. The veil is thinner, no doubt and our awareness is more connected. We embody their spirit and their legacies within and through the ways we walk on this earth. Thich Nhat Hanh expresses this embodiment with, "The leaves that remain are only a very small part of the tea. The tea that goes into me is a much bigger part of the tea. It is the richest part. We are the same; our essence has gone into our children, our friends, and the entire universe. We have to find ourselves in those directions and not in the spent tea leaves."

Bye, Felicia

I mention a crumbling over and over again in this chapter. If you haven't been living in a cave, well actually even if you live in a straight up cave (and I've met modern folks who have and do on this island), you can certainly feel perhaps in even deeper levels what's occurring in the world at large — it's hitting the fan on all areas of our earth experience. The Sages call it "the quickening" and "the Great Shift." Systems, structures, rules, and beliefs are not only showing their cracks, they are cracking with a bang. You can feel that these old systems are in their last throes, like when you watch an animal dying. I wince as I use that analogy, as one of the biggest heart breaks of this Great Shift is the loss and death of so many animals on land, in the air and in the sea. But just like a dying animal, grasping at life and doing what it can to get its last breath, so are the systems that are near their end too. It is getting more frantic, frenetic and chaotic, it seems.

This is where our practice of conscious breathing, conscious dreaming and manifesting, compassionate communication, crystal clear honesty and discernment, intentional actions, brave vulnerability and awakened presence — the whole bag of Jedi Magic Tricks pretty much — must be now put into use as we anchor in the new consciousness and awareness that will take the place of the old dying systems that are harmful and disharmonic to life and love.

"Bye, Felicia" is a term made famous by Ice Cube as a "dismissive kiss-off" (as the urban dictionaries define it). We may not have the time or energy to spend in fighting the old systems that are crumbling although dismantling them together is our responsibility because every single human on this planet somehow or another has benefited from this unsustainable and destructive system and co-created it with our limited consciousness. The most potent way of dismantling these systems is through divesting our resources, energy, presence, allegiance, loyalty, dependence and super powers from them. And reinvesting them into what we are creating that is new.

I had the pleasure of seeing Marianne Williamson at the 2019 Conscious Life Expo in Los Angeles. She is a model of spiritual activism, shining the spotlight on the American shadows and willing to dismantle these structures from the ground up and in turn create new structures infused with spiritual awareness and inter-connectivity. She is running for President of the United States. Although many think it's a long shot, she is the one candidate I am listening to the most, because she gets the psychic and soul surgery needed for America to heal. On stage, she said:

> *"There is a point in everyone's spiritual journey where, if you are not careful, the search for self-awareness can turn into self-preoccupation. There is a fine line, at times, between self-exploration and narcissism. One way to see how we're doing is to measure the fun factor: spiritual growth that's too much fun all the time usually isn't growth at all. Anything that has become too comfortable cannot ultimately be comforting. The universe is invested in our healing, and healing is a fierce, transformative fire. It is the product of human willingness to change, and change is often hard.*
>
> *For years, I thought I only had to heal myself, and the world would take care of itself. Clearly, we must work on healing our own neuroses in order to become effective healers. But then, having worked on our own issues a while, another question bets for an answer: how healed can we ultimately become while the social systems in which we live and move, and have our earthly being, remain sick?*
>
> *World conditions challenge us to look beyond the status quo for responses to the pain of our times. We look to powers within as well as to powers without. A new, spiritually based social activities is beginning to assert itself. It stems not from hating what is wrong and trying to fight it, but from loving what could be and making the commitment to bring it forth. A non-violent political dynamic is once again emerging, and it is a beacon of light*

4: Leave the Old Paradigm

at the dawn of the twenty-first century. The goal, as in the words of Martin Luther King Jr., is "the establishment of the beloved community." Nothing less will heal our hearts and nothing less will heal the world.

It is the task of our generation to recreate the American politeia, to awaken from our culture of distraction and re-engage the process of democracy with soulfulness and hope. Yes, we see there are problems in the world. But we believe in a universal force that, when activated by the human heart, has the power to make all things right. Such is the divine authority of love; to renew the heart, renew the nations, and ultimately, renew the world."

As we divest, dismantle, learn from, and realign ourselves internally in our self-awareness and externally in our communities and organizations in our new paradigm creations, what are we going to create? How? And with whom? As Dr. Martin Luther King, Jr. calls it "the establishment of the beloved community." These are the next questions we will explore in the Luminary's Journey. As we arise from the ashes of an old paradigm burning down, old structures we are consciously dismantling, and create from the compost a thriving New Earth, let us take the incredible medicine and wisdom we have cultivated from the old paradigm (often of the shadows and wounds we are collectively and individually working on within) and create wisely, intentionally, and in service from our hearts. Another goddess politician I am following like a school girl with a crush, is Alexandria Ocasio Cortez. She is using her genius to be a powerhouse presence in Congress — keenly pointing out the cracks in the systems and innovatively proposing solutions like the

Green New Deal. Thank the heavens for Instagram and being able to pretty much go grocery shopping with our modern day super-heroines and watch them assemble IKEA furniture while waxing politics. It's amazing. You really get to know people on intimate levels and see what keeps them up at night and what motivates them to show up, fully, with all of their heart. I predict and pray she will make it to the Presidency one day (when she's old enough — just a few more years and she's eligible — could you believe that?). Pay attention to the women rising in every field across the globe. It's like watching the Pele flow, the embers glowing in the darkness. We are just getting started.

As I mentioned in the beginning of this Chapter as we stand face to face at this basecamp, in awe of the mountain and journey back down before us, I anoint your feet and bow down to you for making it here in the first place. For choosing to be alive, open, willing, and passionate about making a difference with your life. For using your experience and lessons to create something unique and new that this world has yet to see and experience. For putting on your super hero cape and playing the integral role in creating a new paradigm from inside out. That's *big work*. It's radically honest and sobering work. And no one else on this planet will be able to do it and share the gift you are meant to share, manifest the vision you are meant to create, but you. And the remarkable news is, you are not alone. The beehive is full of awakening Luminaries ready to glow up, show up and do the work necessary. That in itself is a cause for celebration.

5: UNPACK YOUR MAGIC

"I break all spells that keep me asleep from my own magic."
~ *Chani Nicholas* ~

"One of the oldest and most generous tricks that the universe plays on human beings is to bury strange jewels within us all, and then stand back to see if we can find them."
~ *Elizabeth Gilbert* ~

Kryptonite and Superpowers

In the superhero world, kryptonite is to be avoided at all costs because it will weaken or possibly even completely take away your super powers. In the healer's/medicine person's world, kryptonite is to be welcomed and held with reverence as close to our hearts as possible, and transmuted into healing gifts and medicine. It is the initiatory Alchemy 101 lesson of a healer in the making. In other words, our wounds, weaknesses, shadows are alchemized into medicine, magic, super powers — ways we can connect to and help serve and alleviate others on the same journey as us, facing the same kryptonite falling into their lives.

We are softened by our wounds. In this milestone, we will unpack our magic and get to know ourselves more intimately. We will perceive our journey with a magician's spectacles, seeing the roadblocks as divine intervention, the monsters and beasts in our lives us divine gate keepers, and seeing our wounds and scars as divine markers of our initiations in embodying the gifts and medicine we will soon share with our loved ones, families, communities and this Earth.

When I had my nervous breakthrough at twenty-five years old and soon found myself volunteering at a retreat in Hawai'i, thinking I must be the only human going through this existential pain and heartache, I stumbled upon the pool with the intention to read and just soak up the sun and figure out the next steps in my life, and to my surprise there were three people amongst the twelve or so sunbathers by the pool, reading Pema Chodron's *When Things Fall Apart*. Were they giving this away at the front desk or something? I had the same book in my bag! How could all of these radiant looking, happy humans on retreat be going through the same annihilation as I am? It was a huge awakening for me to feel connected to this community in that way. I certainly was not alone and seeing people's entranced and focused glowing faces behind this same title just softened me in a kind of vulnerability and openness that I feel was a green light for God to work Her miracles and magic with me — in the guise of synchronistic conversations, accelerated alignment with incredible teachers, reflections from others of exact scenarios they are navigating through, meeting healers that carried the exact medicine that I needed. The moment my belief system switched from "I am all alone" to "Wow, all these people's lives are falling apart too? I have reflections everywhere." my entire life shifted and opened. This is my favorite and most impactful insight from Pema Chodron, and in my humble opinion, should be a (wo)manifesto we read as healers every time we need the reminder:

"Life is glorious, but life is also wretched. It is both. Appreciating the gloriousness inspires us, encourages us, cheers us up, gives us a bigger perspective, energizes us. We feel connected. But if that's all that's happening, we get arrogant and start to look down on others, and there is a sense of making ourselves a big deal and being really serious about it, wanting it to be like that forever. The gloriousness becomes tinged by craving and addiction. On the other hand, wretchedness – life's painful aspect – softens us up considerably. Knowing pain is a very important ingredient of being there for another person. When you are feeling a lot of grief, you can look right into somebody's eyes because you feel you haven't got anything to lose – you're just there. The wretchedness humbles us and softens us, but if we were only wretched, we would all just go down the tubes. We'd be so depressed, discouraged and hopeless that we wouldn't have enough energy to eat an apple. Gloriousness and wretchedness need each other. One inspires us, the other softens us. They go together."

Our capability to become alchemists, magicians, miracle workers and quantum healers in the same caliber as Jesus, Lao Tsu, Quan Yin, Mary Magdalene and these Avatars and Heavenly Superstars is based upon how open and softened we are to not only the realization of Oneness but the *experience* of our Humanness. When every cell of our being recognizes its oneness with every atom and wave of frequency on Earth and within all beings (plants, animals, and humans) we are capable of healing and harmonizing with everything. But for us to experience Oneness, we must really understand our individualized humanness first. And most importantly, we must embrace our wholeness first. That is how Jesus turned water into wine, multiplied bread and fish to feed the masses. That is how Jesus walked on water and healed the sick with a mere gaze, sentence or touch. He experienced this divine empathy and oneness because he self-realized and embraced his individual wholeness first. There needs to be a solid vessel for God to experience Herself through you. That's why we have human bodies and the ego and all the genius mechanisms that make us human. We need the container for spirit to reside in, move through, and experience life from. Jesus was not only filled with the inspiration of the Holy Spirit and the self-realization of his divinity, he was also softened by his human experience of grief, anger, suffering. He felt it all and was able to empathize and see himself within every person he encountered.

Our wounds and the kryptonite that causes them, become our wands and medicine we can use for magic, healing and miracles to help others on the path. As you begin to acknowledge the suffering and pain and shine a light on your wounds, begin to see the lessons, wisdom, experience, and softening you received from them, keep this list in your medicine magic box, for there will be a time when the Universe will tap you on the shoulder to share them with someone who magically appears in front of you. The more softened you are, whole in your humanness, and grounded on this Earth Walk, the more opportunities you will have to share with others, as you devote yourself to be a vessel for this level of divine magic on Earth.

Forgive and Remember the Lesson

Ever since I was a kid, and I felt the burn of friendship betrayal in the playgrounds and classrooms of the Catholic School I went to, the old adage of "forgive and forget" never sat well with me. It was impossible to forget being taunted about my Filipino accent and the way I said certain words. That burned into my memory and heart as that was the first time I experienced racism in my face as a nine-year-old. It wouldn't have served me to hold on to that betrayal all year through fifth grade and plot revengeful comebacks. I do understand why "forgetting" would be more beneficial but I now see in hindsight that instead of "forgive and forget" – much more sound advice would be "forgive and remember the lesson."

Remembering the lesson integrates that experience in a much more effective way and amplifies the wisdom and gifts it brings. I can grow from that experience of racism. I can understand where that came from and what that may reveal about the bully's upbringing, family life, and how that doesn't change my worth at all. In fact, I can learn that my accent makes me unique and being fluent in two languages at nine years old is amazingly beneficial. I can learn about jealousy and understand how that projects from lack of self-worth. I can learn about bullying and judgment and learn how that feels when I'm on the end of that projection which would deter me from judging others and bullying anyone I feel jealous of or insecure around.

There are lists upon lists of lessons if we were to dissect this moment in the playground. Forgiving and then forgetting however, misses the opportunity. Often times we say, "Forgive and forget" with more emphasis on "forgetting" and just "letting it go." But where does it go? Like a boomerang, most events in life that need forgiving, come back around to either test us again to see if we've really learned whatever lesson we needed to learn or it comes back around because we never fully experienced it the first time it presented itself in our life. We avoided the emotions, the lessons, the digestion, the transformation.

Imagine being able to pause, and sit down, and dissect all of these moments that caused wounding in our lives this way, with the intention to forgive and remember the lesson. Not forget, because if we push it out of our consciousness and spiritually bypass these betrayals and wounds that we experience, we lose the opportunity to really learn from them and grow and most likely, they will repeat themselves in our lives because the wound was left unexamined. These unexamined wounds will only magnetize the same experience over and over again until we examine it, glean the lessons and heal it to the core.

There are incredible modalities that help us detangle these stories and experiences that cause us pain to effectively extract the lesson from it before closing the wound. I have found the Ancient Hawaiian practice of ho'oponopono an incredible tool, as well as Systemic Family Constellation Work (which I will dive into more in the next section). Ho'oponopono is a structure set up to create space for everyone's perspective and hurt to be expressed through a facilitator whose primary role is to remain neutral and guide the conversation between the different parties in conflict. The outcome of ho'oponopono is each individual takes accountability for their part in co-creating the conflict. They acknowledge their feelings and are witnessed in the expression of their feelings. They also can acknowledge and witness the feelings of the other person they are in conflict with and a resolution and deeper understanding is awakened in each individual. It's such an effective modality to use that creates the spaciousness and safety to explore the emotions and lessons in these heated moments and initiations. Eventually, the participants of a ho'oponopono arrive at a place and vibration of gratitude for one another – beyond forgiveness even, as they realize what a gift that conflict was for their growth, understanding and healing of the heart. I have to say this as a disclaimer, ho'oponopono has been severely whitewashed by the New Age community. It's even being sold with discounts on Facebook Ads. It is a much deeper process than simply saying *I am sorry. Please forgive me. I love you. Thank you.* This has been a dangerous misconception perpetuating a lot of spiritual bypassing, in my humble opinion. I highly encourage you to find a Native Hawaiian practitioner or a teacher honoring a rooted lineage that can facilitate a holistic and multi-layered ho'oponopono for you if it's needed.

Forgiving and remembering the lesson is an invaluable tool for your growth as a healer, magician, miracle worker and Luminary for you will begin to embrace and willingly lean into every conflict you encounter and every wound you feel – with a perspective that these moments are some of the greatest teachings you'll encounter on your path. In *Emergent Strategies: Shaping Change, Changing Worlds*, adrienne maree brown, in her poetess way expresses this strategy:

"remember you are water. of course you leave salt trails. of course you are crying. flow. p.s. if there happens to be a multitude of griefs upon you, individual and collective, or fast and slow, or small and large, add equal parts of these considerations: that the broken heart can cover more territory. that

perhaps love can only be as large as grief demands. that grief is the growing up of the heart that bursts boundaries like an old skin or a finished life. that grief is gratitude. that water seeks scale, that even your tears seek the recognition of community. that the heart is a front line and the fight is to feel in a world of distraction. that death might be the only freedom. that your grief is a worthwhile use of your time. that your body will feel only as much as it is able to. that the ones you grieve may be grieving you. that the sacred comes from the limitations. that you are excellent at loving."

You will learn, dear Luminary, that you are not only excellent at loving but you are a limitless frequency wave of love. Continue to soften, continue to lean in, continue to forgive, but integrate these conflicts like a master alchemist and you'll be *"golden golden golden,"* as Jill Scott sings.

Ancestral Healing and Activations

Connecting to our ancestors, their stories, their dreams, can be one of the most empowering journeys we can go on. It is incredibly grounding to know where you are rooted in your humanness on Earth. Many of us, due to colonization, have gotten cut off from knowledge of our ancestry. It often happens when another country invades your own country, and tells the people that their practices are "savage" or "wrong" and often introduces Christianity. Then often, the laws making speaking your own language illegal are imposed. And once you take a people's language away, you start to disconnect them from their stories.

Many people in the world right now are healing this disconnection from our languages, our ancestral stories, our connectedness to how our ancestors thrived, healed and lived in harmony with the earth. In my own self-healing and in my healing services for others, it has become apparent that this is some of the greatest and deepest work we can do in the healing of the world, but most especially within our family systems and in ourselves. The journey of Ancestral Healing ignites our ancient memories. These ancient memories, imbedded in our etheric and physical DNA, can literally move mountains and usher in a golden age, times of enlightenment our ancient ancestors have known and have passed down through our lineage to us.

Scientists, through the study of epigenetics, have proven what the Sages and indigenous cultures around the world have always been practicing and sharing, that our DNA carries the memories of our Ancestors. Beyond the physiological and chemical characteristics and traits that our chromosomes carry, there is also an imprint of memory that our ancestors have passed down in the DNA we have within. These memories get activated sometimes spontaneously but often times something in our life experience triggers these memories. For the awakened black sheep healer visionary of the family (that is you, dear Luminary) it becomes part of your super power inheritance and responsibility to acknowledge these activated memories, resolve and heal them for not only the liberation of your Ancestor and his/her karma in this Earth Walk and Incarnation Cycle but also the liberation of yourself and your entire lineage, past, present, and future. And it is also your responsibility, to take the genius and wisdom from these remembrances and embody them, use them, share them to help elevate the human experience on Earth. I know, it's a lot. But we are actually more than prepared and resourced for this.

The most efficient modality I've ever come across that can address ancestral healing and empowerment without having to spend years in processing stories, is Systemic Family Constellation work. We have hosted Anutosh Foo and Francesca Mason Boring here at the center who have generously bridged this ancient practice here to Hawai'i and our community. This work is inspired by the Zulu Tribes in Africa and developed by German therapist Bert Hellinger. Francesca Mason Boring is a Shoshone Elder who helped reframe this ancient practice rooted in Africa back to a ceremonial and ritualistic way. She is gentle and honoring in her practice yet so penetratingly precise. I am so grateful that she has blessed Hawai'i twice now in her facilitation and teachings. I highly recommend this modality with every client I serve and work with as it is the most efficient, quantum way of healing, understanding, forgiving, releasing, and transforming of our ancestral karma, wounds and mysteries. It gives us the ability to time travel and quantumly heal our DNA and the memories they carry across space and time. This modality is a major magic tool to have in your medicine magic box for yourself, your family and your clients.

As we continue to bridge ourselves, families, communities and clients we serve through this Great Shift, it is integral to acknowledge our matriarchal and patriarchal lineages for the gifts they have given us. There is plenty to heal within these lineages and plenty of wisdom and medicine to embody too. As Kazu Haga proposes, "If we carry intergeneration trauma (and we do), then we also carry intergeneration wisdom."

Our lineages go back to the most ancient of times, connecting us to the very first humans and civilizations that have come before us. As we come full circle and deepen the spiral of our evolution we are returning to a matriarchal world deeply connecting to the matriarchal feminine force of creation and Planet Earth. This teaching by Ananda Karunesh in *A Thousand Seeds of Joy: Teachings of Lakshmi and Saraswati* encompasses the Mother's Heart that as healers, be it if we identify as women, men or transgendered and non-binary, we are tapping into every time we create space for our loved ones, families, communities, and clients to heal. I'll leave this quote with you, as an empowerment and activation to remember this within yourself:

"A 'matriarchal world' does not mean matrilineal or that one queen shall rule the world. It simply means a world in which a Mother's Heart leads all social institutions, corporations, and governments. All humans- men, women, or transgender- can embody a mother's heart if they so choose. We are destined for extinction as a human race unless a mother's heart assumes leadership of the world."

Kundalini Rising and Grounding

Kundalini is a Sanskrit word meaning "coiled hair." In many spiritual traditions around the world it is often depicted as a coiled snake that can spring and rise up the spine, activating our chakras also known as spinning wheels of energetic light. You can often feel this buzzing at the base of your spine when your Kundalini is activated. The sensation of it rising up your spine can feel like heat, like tingles and the effects are extraordinary – you feel as if you have a lightning rod at times of connection to God and your Higher Self. You feel clearer, vital, energized, aligned and divine. Some people have a gradual awakening which is ideal. As this type of energy is the greatest force we carry and if activated too soon, or too potently it can cause your nervous system to short circuit. I've read an article once that stated how a group of shamans were once asked about patients in a psychiatric ward and they said that 90% of these patients simply had their Kundalini Energy activated without the proper inner tools and capabilities to create space for and ground these energies back to their bodies. In other words, it short-circuited their brains and nervous system. I believe it.

Gopi Krishna is well known as one of the first people to actually write down his experience of a Kundalini Awakening in the 1950s when this information was not widely spoken about. Wisdom from Kundalini Yoga and Kriyas were often kept hidden from commoners and only shared with royalty and trained devotees of Yogi and Yogini Masters. To Gopi Krishna's surprise and bewilderment he experienced a spontaneous Kundalini Awakening and grounded himself enough to write about it:

"Little did I realize that from that day onward I was never to be my old normal self again, that I had unwittingly and without preparation or even adequate knowledge of it roused to activity the most wonderful and stern power in man, that I had stepped unknowingly upon the key to the most guarded secret of the ancients, and that henceforth for a long time I had to live suspended by a thread, swinging between life on the one hand and death on the other, between sanity and insanity, between light and darkness, between heaven and earth."

In my own personal journey and initiations through the Kundalini Yoga lineage taught by Yogi Bhajan, I could definitely relate to Gopi Krishna's experience and depiction of living "suspended by a thread, between sanity and insanity, light and darkness, heaven and earth." Imagine yourself a coil of the most powerful energy in the world within your body – an energetic slinky of sorts – without structure, discipline and guidance to ground that energy, it can be very disorientating. Another resonating expression of this kundalini force and its disorienting power is sound healing and multi-dimensional channel Tom Kenyon's documentary "Song of the New Earth." He narrated the story of his Kundalini Awakening in college and the gifts he started to realize he had soon after his awakening.

You have most likely experienced a Kundalini Awakening in subtle and for some of you not so subtle ways. I encourage you to find resonating practices that will help ground this cosmic energy back down your body, stabilizing it within yourself, and therefore allowing you to continue to channel this divine guidance and frequency into Earth. Especially as solar flares and huge energetic shifts continue to hit Earth as our poles shift and all kinds of intergalactic and earthly phenomena begin to happen more frequently. Our nervous systems do need to be prepared. Because that is what we are here for … it is not to ascend prematurely and leave this dimension but to in fact, anchor in that divine frequency, that heavenly inspiration onto this Earth plane in an authentically embodied way. Get grounded. The deeper your roots can grow in the earth, the more expansive and higher your branches can grow.

One of my greatest teachers on O'ahu is Dr. Lillian Chang. She brought acupuncture to Hawai'i and is the 64th Lineage Wisdom Holder from Longhushan (Dragon Tiger Mountain), the mountain that Lao Tsu was from. She once did a treatment on me, and by simply looking at my palm, reading my pulse and observing me for less than a few minutes, she said, "all branches, no roots." I was 32 years old then. I was on O'ahu just beginning to come back to the world after scaling the mountain top of spiritual seeking and training. I was working in Waikiki as a massage therapist at the Royal Hawaiian Hotel and going to school for Chinese Medicine. I thought I was the most grounded I've been in a while and this was an incredible wakeup call from Shihfu.

"Strengthen your trunk," she said, "and deepen your roots, so your branches can…" and she waved her arms sporadically and stretched them to the sky. And she walked away. Her signature move is to blow your mind with a very precise and direct wisdom and walk away. I kept that advice close to my heart and continued to work on grounding myself back to Earth, and finding ways to set down some roots. I knew that someday for this healing center to manifest, I would have to stay put somewhere long enough for my roots to settle and stretch.

Physical activities like hiking in forests, running, yoga focused on your core, dance also focused on your core, hips and legs, centering meditation, gardening and earthing (walking barefoot) are all incredible immediate actions to ground back on Earth. Often times, the experience of awakening and shooting up into these higher realms of being can be so blissful that coming back down to our bodies and our earthly day-to-day experiences can be a total buzz kill and very shocking. It is not uncommon to have resistance to grounding. I know, I've most definitely clung to those higher realms of bliss too from time to time. But eventually you realize, this whole heaven on earth gig that we signed up for, well, that can only be accomplished if we come back from those blissful experiences of nirvana and anchor it in to our daily lives. Otherwise, clinging to those heightened states is like taking off to find medicine to help yourself and your loved ones, finding it at the top of a sacred mountain, being so ecstatic with your experience of finding the medicine then not bringing the medicine back down the mountain to share with others. This is not the time in Earth's history to stay in the cave on mountain tops. We have summited the next level in our human evolution now, dear Luminary. It's all about coming back down the mountain and practicing and sharing your wisdom and medicine with the world. I thank the teachers and elders on my path for helping me come back down the mountain. We are needle points of frequency on this Earth and the goal is, wherever we go, whatever rooms we walk into, and lands we root into, is that we can embody that frequency and bring heaven into reality through our actions, words and authentic being.

It helps incredibly to take care of your body as it is the vessel that will carry these new frequencies you are activating when you reach those heights and ride that cosmic serpent of energy. Your body will tell you exactly what it needs to shift and be a more vital vessel for these higher frequencies. It will tell you through allergies, food preferences, the type of activities it wants to experience, exercise and movement that its craving, and sometimes a healing crisis to shine a light on the disharmony to bring itself back into alignment and balance. More than ever, at this stage of your journey as a Luminary, when you are reaching new heights of consciousness and awareness you have yet to experience before, it is integral to pay so much more attention to your body, this incredible vessel that holds your divinity and magic to be expressed here on Earth. Your body and its ability to integrate your magic is an integral relationship you must continue to develop throughout your entire life, dear Luminary. This is embodied spirituality. This is being a living human avatar.

Real Life Hogwarts

Speaking of Kundalini Awakenings, one of the most modern and visible people who underwent a Kundalini Awakening in public is Russel Brand, the British Comedian. He battled heroin addiction, alcoholism, and deep depression with Kundalini Yoga and practices it daily. When I became aware of his practice, I started to pay more attention to him in his public life and I've got to say how utterly inspired I am with his perspective and expression. If you haven't seen his work, YouTube him and watch him wax poetic on everything under the sun. His interview with the Dalai Lama is wonderful too. His most recent book is called *Mentors*. In it, he speaks of his teachers from AA to the healers and teachers in his path as a seeker. He serves us spirituality with a real authentic and hilarious edge.

When it comes to finding your mentors, teachers and guides, Russel Brand says, "If you don't choose your own heroes, heroes will be chosen for you, and they will not represent values that empower you, they will represent powers that will enslave you." Oh yes. This is absolute truth. As magicians, healers and luminaries, mentorship is key to our growth and maturity. It keeps us honest, grounded, and embodied. The days of the guru and putting them on pedestals are quickly disappearing into the dust of the old paradigm. Many are being dethroned right now too. Their humanness and shadows are being revealed and alas we realize that they are human after all, and they too have shadows they work with and they too have really bad days and meltdowns and they too question God and throw their fists up in the air denouncing the cruelty and unfairness of the heavens. Sometimes, these gurus and teachers we have put on pedestals feel even more trapped in their spiritual identities and have unfortunately perfected the art of spiritual bypassing. They run from their shadows faster than we do. So before seeking out and devoting yourself to teachers, mentors and guides, remind yourself they are human and be aware of your tendency to need to idolize other humans. Perhaps you are projecting certain needs, often stemming from the nourishing and disciplining dynamics you experienced as a child. It's very wise to go into mentorship with your eyes wide open and your self-awareness very centered within your being.

Sharpen your discernment and look for mentors, teachers and guides who embody their wholeness and humanness – you will know that by their authenticity and often, ridiculous sense of humor. Case in point – the Dalai Lama. At a talk he was giving in Honolulu a few years ago, an audience member asked him if he ever frowned or ever felt not compelled to smile or be happy, as it seems that he's always smiling. His interpreter asked the question and patiently waited for his answer, as he took a moment and long pause to really ponder this question. We all sat in anticipation for what he would choose to say – perhaps he would point out some atrocity happening around the world, the violent Chinese military occupation of Tibet maybe, and when he answered, his interpreter turned crimson and couldn't stop laughing. When he finally was able to gather himself together and interpret what His Holiness said, he uttered three simple words, "on the toilet." The Dalai Lama said he doesn't smile when he's on the toilet. That is wisdom, humility, humor, and honesty all balled up in one. We all broke out in laughter. I have found my most embodied teachers who walk the talk and see me clearly (because they see themselves super clearly) and accept me with so much nourishment and love and yet also dish it out with fiercely pointed wisdom are the ones who also make me laugh so hard my cheeks hurt.

Soon enough, if not already, you will also come to realize that everyone you encounter is a teacher. We are always learning from one another and teaching one another too. If we can put on our magical spectacles more and experience life as if it is Hogwarts, we can continue to stretch our capacity to receive the support and wisdom from God at every turn. Because it is there but often times, we are so caught up in our navel gazing ways, we miss the incredible opportunities, reflections, symbols, signs and support we are surrounded with.

In the cosmic viewpoint of life, it really isn't that serious. This is an Earth School which we all willingly and consciously signed up for. Some of us chose really challenging curriculums and some of us make it more challenging than it should be, but nevertheless, find the teachers, mentors and guides that will help you hone your magic, be honest with you and empower self-correction, inspire you by not only their words but by how they embody their teachings through vulnerability, transparency, generosity, and endless compassion. If they can elicit snorting laughter, especially during some challenging moments of existential confusion or deep physical pain – even better, these are Magicians you want in your corner.

6: MAKE YOUR MEDICINE

"If you come to me as a victim I will not support you.
But I will have the courage to walk with you through the pain
that you are suffering.
I will put you in the fire, I will undress you,
and I will sit you on the earth.
I will bathe you with herbs, I will purge you, and you will
vomit the rage and the darkness inside you.
I'll bang your body with good herbs, and I'll put you to lay in
the grass, face up to the sky.
Then I will blow your crown to clean the old memories that
make you repeat the same behavior.
I will blow your forehead to scare away the thoughts
that cloud your vision.
I will blow your throat to release the knot
that won't let you talk.
I will blow your heart to scare fear, so that it goes far away
where it cannot find you.
I will blow your solar plexus to extinguish the fire of the hell you
carry inside, and you will know peace.
I will blow with fire your belly to burn the attachments, and the

love that was not.
I will blow away the lovers that left you,
the children that never came.
I will blow your heart to make you warm, to rekindle your
desire to feel, create, and start again.
I will blow with force your vagina or your penis,
to clean the sexual door to your soul.
I will blow away the garbage that you collected trying to love
what did not wanted to be loved.
I will use the broom, and the sponge, and the rag,
and safely clean all the bitterness inside you.
I will blow your hands to destroy the ties that prevent
you from creating.
I will blow your feet to dust and erase the footprints memories,
so you can never return to that bad place.
I will turn your body, so your face will kiss the earth.
I'll blow your spine from the root to the neck to increase your
strength and help you walk upright.
And I will let you rest.

After this you will cry, and after crying you will sleep,
And you will dream beautiful and meaningful dreams,
and when you wake up I'll be waiting for you.
I will smile at you, and you will smile back
I will offer you food that you will eat with pleasure,
tasting life, and I will thank you.
Because what I'm offering today, was offered to me before when
darkness lived within me.
And after I was healed, I felt the darkness leaving, and I cried.

Then we will walk together, and I will show you my garden,
and my plants, and I will take you to the fire again.
And will talk together in a single voice with
the blessing of the earth.
And we will shout to the forest the desires of your heart.
And the fire will listen and whisper the echo, and we will
create hope together.
And the mountains will listen and whisper the echo, and we
will create hope together.
And the rivers will listen and whisper the echo, and we will
create hope together.
And the wind will listen and whisper the echo, and we will
create hope together.
And then we will bow before the fire, and we will call upon all
the visible and invisible guardians.
And you will say thank you to all of them.
And you will say thank you to yourself.
And you will say thank you to yourself.
And you will say thank you to yourself."

- Author Unknown -

Casting Spells

There is a magical force that ignites and ripples out into the Universe when your dreams, thoughts, intentions, and feelings around this vision is put onto paper, spoken out loud, and allowed to be seen in a tangible blueprint. This is a key lesson in Co-Creation with God 101.

Whether or not you have been in private practice for twenty years already or just recently graduated from a healing arts school, this milestone in your Luminary Journey is an exciting opportunity to fully envision your healing offerings, clients, colleagues, space, and flow. This is where we invite the Visionary Self within you to take the lead and create a wish list (one of several we will do in this Luminary's Journey) which is a love letter to the Universe, your Higher Self, your Future Clients, your Colleagues, your Supporters and Investors and all of the other collaborators destined to bless your path on this journey. This is the first alchemical step in taking your vision and making it into a reality. We will begin by bringing form to your magic.

We were once hosting a retreat here called Tandaan (meaning "to remember" in Tagalog) and all of the facilitators and participants were caravanning to the Warm Ponds in Kapoho on the South East side of the island. These Warm Ponds were one of the many sacred gathering places and natural wonders here on the Big Island that have since been covered up by the lava during the eruption last year in 2018.

I had my dear friend and mambatok, a traditional Filipino tattoo artist, Lane Wilcken, riding shotgun. Lane is also a linguist, teacher, father and author. He has the deep booming voice of a Filipino/Viking (his ancestry and mix and we also joke he's got a bit of Werewolf in his genes because of his fangs). Needless to say when he speaks, you listen, not just because of the depth of his voice but the masterful way he weaves together legends, magic, and the origins of words. For some reason, we were talking about the English language and how it is dead and lost its magic in comparison to other rich languages like the Hawaiian language where you utter one word and your entire body can light up on fire and heat. He mentioned how the alphabet in the English language was altered intentionally to take away its magic. Like the word L-o-v-e … it doesn't really look like that. It's a bit turned around and the letters have been altered. Say whaaa, Lane? He then said, yes, that's why it's called "Spelling." Originally, letters in their original forms had magic infused into them and when strung together into words to create spells. And just like that, my mind bloomed into flowers on the drive. Imagine the possibilities of knowing the original symbols and being able to use them?

With that said, I believe even if this English language was altered in its letters and symbology to neutralize its potency, we can infuse the magic back into it with our intentions, with all the feels vibrating from within us as we envision our offerings. Don't ever doubt that this is a magical act.

This is by far, my favorite part of the process. Let the Visionary inside you run amok and free. This is the time to really take every single initiation, lesson, and gift you've uncovered on the mountain tops you've climbed to and bridge them into offerings and services to benefit others on the journey. What a blessing of an opportunity this is. Be sure to give thanks, even a quantum one through the ethers to all of your teachers along the way who have shared their wisdom and medicine with you. This is what they have envisioned in their hearts blossoming into reality. I am often over-brimming with gratitude when I am in this phase of creating. Gratitude is an incredible energetic space to be in while creating this list. It will infuse these words with more magic than they can handle. Enjoy the process.

The What

Let's begin with your offerings. List all of the gifts and wisdom you carry and create a bucket list of everything. Once you have this list, start to categorize them and see which modalities/wisdom teachings may be harmonious together. Which ones complement one another and which ones can stand on their own? Think of your teachers as well and fellow colleagues, for they can also be folks you invite to your healing center to share their wisdom and healing modalities with the clients you will be serving.

Start to create a menu. You can simply write these down on a notebook or type it up on your computer. The most important part is the thoroughness of this list and the exercise of truly seeing yourself clearly and the gifts of healing, transformation and wisdom you carry and the incredible network of teachers and colleagues who make up the healing village. Write down their gifts and wisdom next to their names. If you're not so sure, make a note to connect to them in the near future and learn about their offerings and medicine.

This will be your magic list of offerings from healing modalities you can offer to retreats and workshops by other colleagues you plan to host at your healing center. If you're drawing a blank at this milestone, or have a feeling that you're missing something or someone, think back to the last milestone and chapter of *Unpack Your Magic*, and scan through your life from childhood and on, also scan your ancestry, scan your teachers and colleagues/healers along the way and ask the gifts and people to illuminate themselves. Write down what comes into the light. You will be awed at how many gifts you carry and the wealth of a gifted and generous community you have met along your journey. The Healer's Path is always full of opportunities to learn and activate your remembrance and super powers.

The Who

You will serve many people with your offerings. People you won't even be able to imagine at this stage. But begin anyway and create another bucket list of people you have already helped (could be short list of siblings, friends, parents, fellow students you just graduated with from healing arts school) or it could be hundreds and thousands of people in your 20-year career. If you're in the hundreds and thousands bracket, you certainly don't have to list every single person, but simply categorize them by demographics and the reasons they sought out your help.

You may see common denominator characteristics, ailments/disharmonies and demographics surface from this list or they can truly run an entire spectrum of folks and reasons. If patterns do come up, take note of them as you highlight certain offerings to cater to this obvious type of client or need.

You can also use these highlighted patterns in the future for marketing purposes. But for now, envision all of the clients you see serving, allow your intuition to guide you. Remember, this healing center of yours and offerings are already existing in a parallel reality and clients are already benefiting from your services, allow yourself to do a bit of time-traveling right now and observe the people waiting in the waiting room, doing an intake with you or your staff, enjoying the treatments and diving deep with your modalities, and leaving your healing space glowing, lighter, happier and maybe even in tears of gratitude.

Now imagine other practitioners you want to work with (whether it is sharing a space with them, or employing them, or they are colleagues you refer clients to and receive referrals from). If you don't have particular people in mind, imagine their qualities (their expertise, their bed side manner, how you feel around them, the sound of their voice, their aesthetic and energy). Time-travel to moments where you see them between sessions and you're discussing their experience with each client and how they are feeling in the space, and flow of their offerings. See them also glowing and radiant full of gratitude because they are able to do what they love in an incredible space and their gifts are shining and making a difference in other's lives.

These moments you are seeing is what you're doing all of this for. All of the initiations, challenges, blood, sweat, and tears will all be worth it when you witness the transformation, healing and joy of someone you have touched and blessed with your presence, medicine and service.

As you create these lists and begin to get used to envisioning the details of the healing center you are also beginning to exercise your manifestation muscles. One of the core muscles you are exercising here if the Manifestation Muscle of Feeling. When you can feel the harmony within you, when you feel the radiating joy, when you can feel the wellness being cultivated in your healing retreat center, it convinces your subconscious mind that it already is happening. Our subconscious cannot tell if something is literally physically happening in your reality already or if it is in the imaginal realm. All it can sense is how you are feeling and the vibration and frequency of these feelings within every cell of your body. There is an actual neurological purpose in infusing your visions with feeling – and this is it. Once we can get our subconscious on board, our ability to manifest our visions into reality can be much more accelerated.

The Why

Let's go deeper in this time-traveling meditation. Let's travel back to the moment you realized you had healing gifts within you. In the last two chapters we left an old paradigm and unpacked the lessons, wisdom, initiations turning your wounds into medicine. Let's wind this clock back even further and go to the time before you even chose your parents and entered your mother's womb. You were this incredibly free and cosmic soul campaigning for admission into Earth School. Can you remember that time right now? What do you see in your observation of Earth School? What do you remember in conversation with Source? If God asked, why do you want to incarnate on Earth? What are you going to do there? What do you want to learn? Can you remember what you said? If you do, write it down. This is the core of your healing center, your North Star.

If you can't see it or hear it just yet, it's alright, you can go back to this time-traveling point in time soon again. Place it in the back of your mind and allow it to explore in its own time and pace. If pre-incarnation is a bit too far back to travel to today, let's go back to childhood, to the time where you were so fascinated and enthralled with a project, show/movie, book, hero/heroine – in other words, what were you into? Like, really, really, *really* into? What were your daydreams like? What did you obsessively ask questions about? What made you so happy and delighted to do? What kept you from doing your homework? What got you in trouble because you couldn't listen to adult rules if it impeded upon the pure joy of doing what you were doing that suspended time and space?

For me, I obsessively created palaces and temples using my Care Bears and other dolls and stuffed animals and gave them all roles to play and directed their interactions in my temple/palace/queendom. There was a lot of complex (for a seven-year-old) situations happening that needed resolution and Care Bear Therapy. I also was obsessed with taking hard back books, and creating futuristic contraptions/secret magical devices with them. I think I was inspired by Penny and Inspector Gadget, but I truly believe I created the first iPad at 1985 and wish fate had connected me to Steve Jobs or Silicon Valley then. Do you see where I'm getting to?

We came into this Earth with these seeds of genius already within us. We already knew what gifts, wisdom, and creations we will be offering into this world. Ironically and often, education in the old paradigm oppresses and programs that genius right out of us. Why was I so obsessed with temples and Care Bear drama and resolution at seven? Was I a budding World Peace Ambassador or Family Conflict Therapist? Was I a Queen in waiting ready for my Empire to be built? Was I a Temple Keeper ready to design utopic communities in the world? Was I a Quantum Physicist inventing Bio Resonance Therapy Gadgets and Sound Healing Machines? Yes and then some. Our inner-child, more than anyone in the world, knows the what, who, why, how, where and when of our gifts. Our gifts are not something to receive from the outside, we were born with them and they make themselves known by what brings us absolute joy. They also make themselves known by the trials and tribulations we endure and not only survive, but rise from them like the phoenixes we are. Usually, our fascinations when we were children are clear indicators of where to explore and unearth our divine genius.

Why are you the way you are? What has been blossoming within you since you were in utero? What is this magnetic energetic force pulling you into being and participating fully in this world? My late and beloved teacher Sobonfu Somé from Burkina Faso once told a story of how her tribe, the Dagara Tribe, welcome babies into the world. They create a song for the baby while she is still in utero, essentially asking the baby to communicate with the tribe and tell them who she is and what she came to Earth to do. When Sobonfu was in her mother's womb, she told her tribe, she would have a big mouth and have a gift of talking. They knew then that she was a bridger, a teacher that will spread the wisdom of their culture and practice to the world.

The village prepared for Sobonfu to be born and therefore knew how to cultivate and nourish her so she can fully embody her gifts. They sang this song they have co-created with her during her birth. They sang it during pivotal moments of her rites of passage. They sang it to her when she sometimes strayed and lost her way, to remind her of who she was and what she said she was here to do. These stories by Sobonfu and of course the way she told them in her mesmerizing voice and incredible humor, just opened my heart to the unlimited possibilities of this ritual and protocol. Could you imagine how humanity would be like, if we sung to and listened to the souls being birthed into our families and communities for the prime reason of learning what their gifts are and how we can prepare ourselves to support that? We would cultivate the genius in each other throughout our lives and understand how integral it is to remind each other of our genius as we evolve.

Connecting to your naturally born gifts and therefore the *why* of your offerings infuses your services with the magic that will get you through every initiation, test and challenge that most people would use as a reason to give up. Your why, will help you persevere and rise. Develop a close relationship with your inner child, the one creating temples in walk-in closets with her Care Bears and turning old dusty books into futuristic innovations that solve mysteries and heal her dolls. She will talk you through those dark nights of the soul when you question everything you're doing and think you may not be up for the challenge.

As one of my favorite embodied humans, Oprah Winfrey says, "The key to realizing a dream is to focus not on success but on significance – and then even the small steps and little victories along your path will take on grater meaning." This too. The victories, little milestone that people don't see, the big leaps of faith you take within you … they will weave a tapestry of legendary proportions of a soul, who came to Earth, to make ripples and waves with her gifts, visions, medicine and life. It starts with the Why. Why are you so compelled to do this?

Dr. Wayne Dyer says it simply, "You create your thoughts, your thoughts create your intentions, and your intentions create your reality."

The How

You are a curator of transformation. From the moment your clients, colleagues, and hosted wisdom keepers walk into the door they are entering a space of healing and transformation you have created. Often when clients come in, they are in a very vulnerable and open space. If some are in deep pain, they may have a coat of armor on that may take some nourishment, gentility and warmth to encourage them to take it off.

Go back to your list of clients, colleagues, teachers you imagined and let's time-travel again to a not-so-distant future on a typical Thursday at the healing center. Walk in and see your appointment book. Is it written down on a calendar, or an app on your phone, pad, or computer?

Is there an intake form on hand or in the computer your clients have filled out so you can quickly see what you're creating healing space for? Who greets them? Is there a waiting room? What refreshments/snacks do you have in the waiting room? What reading materials and information/protocol/forms do you have them read and sign before their sessions? Are there experiences or extra modalities they can experience before they see you while they are waiting? For us here at the center, we have a sauna/steam room and cold plunge salt water pool for clients to enjoy before receiving their healing treatments with us. Is there music? What kind of music and how is it playing throughout the center? What's the intake protocol like when they first enter the room? What is the flow and timing like? How do you want them to experience the treatments? If it's a string of modalities together, what's the most ideal flow? What is the post-treatment protocol look like? Do you provide tea or something to help ground them before they leave and return back in the world? Is there discussion and consultation about the session? Is there a follow-up call or email sent to the client to check in on them? How are you going to host retreats and wisdom keepers? Where is the gathering space? What is a typical flow for a three-day retreat? What are the topics people are learning? What are the takeaways the attendees are so thrilled about?

You will be able to develop your protocols when you imagine the client's journey and experience from the moment they look for your services or workshops, find you and make their first appointment to when they arrive home and integrate the session or retreat throughout the rest of the month. As the saying goes, God is in the details and when it comes to curating a healing and transformative experience, the intention and attention to the protocols and details can truly create a potent space for healing and transformation.

The Where

The space and land where your center will be in is the container and sacred space you are creating to hold the healing and transformative experience you are co-creating with God, your ancestors, your colleagues and clients.

What you are offering, who you are serving and working with, why you are creating this offering, and how you want the experience to be like are all components in choosing a space or land for your healing center to be created.

Sometimes it's a very conscious choice and decision. And sometimes the land and space chooses you and completely surprises you. For me, the volcano and the goddess Pelehonuamea seemed to be conspiring with the Universe and my Ancestors to bring me here in Volcano. It's usually a bit of both — a conscious choice and a deep magnetic pull, a string of synchronicities and divine appointments not under your conscious control whatsoever.

When you have found the space or land, it is important to learn about it. Who are the original inhabitants? What ancestors and cultures were born, lived and died in that space or land? Is there any healing, resolution or clearing you need to do to honor, bring balance to, and cleanse the space or land? What was that space or land originally used for? These inquiries may lead you into fascinating information and connection to why you may personally be called to create a healing center there.

If you are looking to create a healing center on land that is not originally where your ancestors are from, then it is a responsibility and sacred opportunity to ask permission from Spirit and the Ancestors of that land, and most especially learn as much as you can about that land and space and the people, animals and plants who have inhabited it. It connects you in much deeper layers. You know what and who is nourishing your roots. And most importantly you know what ancestors you are honoring and healing with your service.

Spend a lot of time on the land and space and connect to this energy. Often in dreams, I receive messages from Spirit and Ancestors about the land. Upon landing here in Volcano and in our five years of creating the healing center and gardens, several divine interventions occurred that led me to learn more about this space and receive pertinent information that helped shape and create our ceremonies and offerings.

We once had an incredible kumu visit who was a Hawaiian chanter from Molokai. He was known to be able to chant through mountains. I first had the tingling chicken skin honor to hear his chant at the Kīlauea crater in Volcano National Park and one moon later when he had stopped by and attuned us all at the center with his chanting (in many different languages from Hawaiian to Tibetan to unknown light languages). I recognized his voice and was awe struck at the synchronicity. His visit and presence brought attention to the Spirit Guardians and Ancestors of the land who were introducing themselves to him. He genuinely smiled and acknowledged them and even had conversations with them. He also shared his vision of what he saw in the future here, different structures that fascinated him and the excitement and blessing it ignited within his heart. It was such a gift to receive his wisdom and vision.

We've hosted many medicine women and men who have the gift of vision here. We have learned of the vision that this land was once an ancient Hawaiian school that taught magic and metaphysical healing modalities before the eruption of Mauna Loa covering this ancient school. This center is now on top of that. My former wife and I have had dreams here connecting to that time and it brings me to tears whenever I think about how profound that connection is. The guardian and kumu of that ancient school often shows himself to people with the gift of clairvoyance here. He has a commanding presence, over seven feet tall, a mahu, a two-spirited healer and kumu, watchful and regal.

On a more practical and grounded level, a client we once hosted happened to be speaking to her friend randomly on the Kona side, a former Hollywood photographer of the stars and now palm tree aficionado and grower. He realized, over the phone, that he actually grew up on this land. He knew the previous family who lived here and he also knew every single tree planted on this land. He shared that one of the biggest trees we have on this land, a giant maple tree, was gifted to this family by his father, as a seed from Chicago of all places, the city I grew up in.

The space, the land, the Ancestors, and Spirit will have an interesting way in bringing these signs and information to you. Ask. Be curious. And be open to receive. Know the indigenous elders and family guardians of the land you are on and develop a relationship with them learning about the spirit, ecology, culture, and inhabitants of the land. Meet your neighbors as well and do some digging at the public library or land resource departments in your town. You will be guided to learn the pertinent information you need especially if you are genuinely wanting to know.

Ask for permission to be there from Spirit. Ask for the support, guidance, protection, and grace. State your intentions to the land and space. Listen deeply to what the land and Ancestors may be guiding you to create. Create a blessings ceremony to consecrate the space. The level of intention that you create with your relationship with the land and space that holds you is up to you. I encourage you to develop and cultivate a nourishing and deep relationship.

In this age, especially in the West, when a majority of us no longer live on the land we were born on or from where our Ancestors lived, we create homes and communities on land that was likely colonized, illegally and violently occupied and developed. It is our responsibility as Luminaries to illuminate those histories as well and honor the land, culture, spiritual protocols, ecological protocols and the people who originally live on the land. This is part of the awakening journey and the dismantling of the old paradigm responsibilities we have and the ushering in of the New Earth.

You are entering an integral relationship, just as important as with your colleagues, collaborators, clients and supporters. It is important to nurture these relations as an Earth Steward with the land you are creating a healing center on and the community you are joining. It is important to be humbled by the land and your role there. It is important to work together with the Spirits and Ancestors, plant beings and animal beings and the community who are also stewards of this land with you. This is foundational in creating harmonic space for healing and transformation to thrive.

You can also explore deeper levels of this understanding and work with geomancy experts tuning into the energetic lines, ley lines, and flow of the land, Feng Shui consultants, sacred geometry architects and designers, permaculture/food forest landscape designers, etc. It's limitless in the scope and scale you'd like to create this space. Work with what you have and be resourceful and sustainable in your creation.

At this point of the envisioning journey, being a temple creating Care Bear Resolution Ambassador that I am, my inner-child goes wild here and I devour books, magazines, design photographs, that inspire me to really open up my imagination and feel into what wants to grow and blossom in this space in harmony with the energies of the land and environment, what we are offering and creating and who we are serving. It's an incredibly exciting process enhanced by the depth of your curiosity and intentions.

The When

I'm no astrologer, but I've certainly lived long enough (especially on this elemental and primal island) to be humbled enough to respect the power of the sun, the moon, the stars and planets and how they affect the elements, the weather, the land, the waters, animals, technology, travel, business contracts, communications, and us humans. I continue to be fascinated by how I can co-exist and be in harmony with nature and the stars. It's become part of my very practical calendar protocol to include the moon cycles, solstices, equinoxes and transits, Mercury Retrogrades, Venus, and Jupiter Retrogrades, and all kinds of other astrological phenomena that seems pertinent for the week, month, or year.

I base my contract signing, retreats, cleanses, travel on these moon cycles and planets because I've learned that I will receive as much help from all the Universal Forces as I can for the graceful flow and organization of this center. It does matter. Aligning myself and the business to the natural and cosmic ebb and flow helps me use the energies in amplifying and enhancing our offerings. It helps me know when to rest and slow down too. It helps me understand when certain retreats will best be held and when marketing these retreats will be most beneficial. It helps me know when certain practices and cleanses will be most supported too and what rituals we can do to help plant intentions, cleanse spaces, honor the ancestors and grow and harvest food.

The Hawaiian Moon Calendar is fascinating in the way that the ancients knew precisely how nature is affected by the moon. I enjoy sitting down with my calendar at the beginning of the year and the month and set it with these extra tools at hand. And rather than attempting to explain this ancient complex technology to you with my elementary understanding, you would be much better off with my referrals to the experts: Chani Nicholas, Lena Stevens of The Power Path, Jessica Dawn Bourque of Temple of the Moon, The Hoodwitch, Mystic Mama, Kaypacha Lescher at New Paradigm Astrology, Navajo Elder and Herbalist Lillian McCracken of Green Earth Farm and Kahu Wendell Kalanikapuaenui Silva and his Hawaiian Mystic Moon Chart are my go to astrological wisdom keepers whom I consult so I know when to launch retreats, hold cleanses, sign documents, go into contracts, book travel, plant certain plants, go to the ocean and howl my prayers at the moon.

Remember that you, yourself, are intuitively and instinctually connected to the cycles of the heavens and the earth. You are made out of stardust after all. You don't *have* to base anything on astrology, it is merely a tool to use if you'd like. The most important tool to use when scheduling retreats, ceremonies, cleanses, plantings, and your business flow is the GPS within your own being. You know best, especially when you have foundationally worked on staying connected to the earth and the Ancestors, your co-creator God and most especially the embodiment of your spirit within your grounded humanness.

7: ILLUMINATE THE SHADOW

"Until we have met the monsters in ourselves, we keep trying to slay them in the outer world. And we find that we cannot. For all darkness in the world stems from darkness in the heart. And it is there that we must do our work.
~ Marianne Williamson ~

Shadow Boxing

A quote I've fallen in love with:

"Sooner or later on this journey, every traveler faces the same question: Are you a human intending to be a god, or a god pretending to be a human?"
~ Eric Micha'el Leventhal ~

What I find so fascinating with this Earth School is the counter-intuitive pre-requisite that we agree to and purposely put blinders on ourselves when we incarnate and enroll. If in fact we are made in the image of God, why do we spend our entire lives trying to remember what we know right before we enter this planet and existence? Why do we script our human characters and give ourselves amnesia? I spent a lot of my young adulthood really mad about this sleight of hand. It seems manipulative and setting us up for failure and an incarnation of confusion.

Life seems like a satire:

The Creator: You're divine and perfect and a magical god/goddess that can manifest anything you want and create any reality you want with the power of your love within you.

We Souls Campaigning to be Humans: What, really? Okay, I'm in. How can we get in on this Earth gig?

The Creator: Just take this blue pill and we'll send you right in.

We Soon-to-be-Humans: (Eagerly swallow pill)

(Light and Energy alchemize into DNA sequences and Human Blueprint is created including time of birth, place of birth, family of birth. The stage is set.)

Stage left: We Humans enter Earth.

Stage right: Enter The Programmers and Social Engineers (a.k.a. other people who took the blue pill and are really hamming up their roles of Fear-Inducing "Bad Guys")

The Programmers: You are bad. You were born a sinner. You are not worthy. You are scandalous. You are not beautiful unless you buy this [fill in the blank]. You are in great danger in this fearful evil world. You cannot love in certain ways. There is something wrong with you if you have feelings. Take this pill to suppress all emotions. And then take this other pill to deal with those side-effects from the first pill. Let's spray this poison on your food, to protect the food from bugs and so we can produce more food and feed more people, and then buy this pill so that you can get better from the poison we sprayed on your food otherwise you will die.

At least it's not from malnourishment but probably because of cancers. Blah, blah, blah ... (trails off in Charlie Brown adult voice)

We Humans: Beam me up, Scotty.

In a twenty-second satire, this is how incarnation can look like. We forget we are divine and enter some kind of vortex of duality. We are bombarded from the moment we enter this existence with messages that we are in fact *not divine* but flawed and divided. That is beginning to change as we all awaken. A different kind of human is entering the planet in a different kind of environment with different kinds of parents who are remembering their divinity more and more and are therefore making sure that their children are protected from the effects of the blue pill.

Perhaps the blue pill is the catalyst of this Earth School to help our souls grow, to help us remember our divinity through the game of amnesia and duality. That's why it's a pre-requisite. We grow, we evolve the human race, we elevate the consciousness of the earth through the built-in programs to challenge us. Could this possibly be what this gig is all about?

The side-effects of this blue pill are these shadows we have within ourselves from the programming, abuse, trauma, and projected pain we acquired from other We Humans who took the blue pill too. They are our lessons waiting to be brought to light. Rather than hate ourselves and be ashamed about these symptoms of the blue pill, we can compassionately heal it and illuminate the lessons. It's part of the curriculum on Earth. It's part of our divine embodiment.

Often, in our spiritual evolution, we become overwhelmed with these shadows because we have been programed to judge ourselves and each other harshly. The Programmers love to use fear as the primary tool to program us. So a reactionary habit we've developed is to bypass them, ignore them, leave them in the darkness and deny their existence within ourselves or even worse we project them on one another. It is so much easier to focus our energy on the shadows of the world and others who we strictly place in the roles of being the "Bad Guys" but extremely more painful to turn the gaze within and face these shadows within ourselves — gently, compassionately and vulnerably. These fears and resistances are up for a paradigm shift. You see, we've cracked the code. We've evolved enough as humanity to remember the contract we signed and the script we created. Our shadows are our greatest lessons for growth and more light. Knowing this, no amount of blue pills can erase that from our embodied human understanding. Not in this stage of our evolution.

The world's destiny does depend on how much light we can shine toward the darkness, internally and externally. The key here is we've got to start doing that for ourselves first and then work ourselves into bigger and darker spaces to shine light on. You are a Luminary after all, and to illuminate the world, you must be willing to first illuminate what's within you.

In other words, as Ice Cube raps, "You better check yourself before you wreck yourself." I believe this is what Ice Cube means: Self-accountability. Self-realization. Self-forgiveness. Self-responsibility. These are all Jedi Super Powers we can practice so we don't self-sabotage.

Luminary, Byron Katie proposes that, "Our parents, our children, our spouses and our friends will continue to press every button we have, until we realize what it is that we don't want to know about ourselves, yet. They will point us to our freedom every time." Liberation is ours, when we can fully embrace our shadows, know them intimately and therefore integrate them in ways which we no longer are ruled by them in our responses to any trigger anyone could ever pull on us. This is The Work, as Byron Katie calls it. It is foundational work before we even begin to create. It's the proverbial weeding of the garden we wish to grow seeds in. It's necessary. It creates an elegant efficiency (as my Systemic Family Constellations teacher Francesca Mason Boring says). And its reward is our sovereignty and joy to consciously live as "gods pretending to be humans." It's a fascinating game and script — we are clever co-conspirators aren't we?

The Paralysis of Perfectionism

Here's another tricky and rapid growing weed that can suffocate a growing plant any given day. Perfectionism. Once again, I'd rather just skip this subject and move right along. I have an intimate love-hate relationship with perfectionism. Love in a sense that I recognize that the Divine is Perfect. Order, beauty, alignment are all qualities of the Divine, I believe and so I love and appreciate perfection. We humans, we feel good when our lives are in order. We feel good when we are feeling ourselves and acknowledging our beauty. And we feel confident and in divine grace when we are in alignment.

How can divine perfection turn into paralysis in our lives then? I believe it does when it's combined with judgment, unforgiveness, control, lack of self-worth — all versions of fear. Fear can turn something divine and pure into suffering real fast. It does that to divine perfection. Some examples of fear sabotaging perfection and turning it into paralysis:

1. Fear of lack: I don't have enough time to complete this and do a perfect job at it. I'm not even going to begin.

2. Fear of judgment: What are they going to think of me if I do this? I'll die if they judge me. I can't do this.

3. Fear of not being good enough: Who do I think I am in even attempting to do this? Why would I even attempt to do a subpar job, when it's been done so much better by so many other people? I'm not even going to attempt this.

The list keeps going. Fear is an ouroboros, a serpent eating its own tail infinitely. It will always find a reason to protect you from what it feels is danger. As it should. But we've got to have a system of checks and balances with fear. We need to be able to asses if the fear of something dangerous coming is actually valid. Often times, it's not even about what's coming or anything remotely dangerous. It's a knee-jerk programmed response to something unhealed, not investigated and ignored. Perhaps even an old belief system left undetected in our consciousness until this very opportunity that triggers it.

How can we liberate our natural and divine embodiment of perfection from fear? We'll have to dive into these old beliefs, unhealed wounds and undetected programs that use fear as their first defense for their survival. Question their validity. Be willing to be real and honest with ourselves. And then begin to create new neuropathways in our brains, by continuing to embrace and be grateful for perfection. Notice it everywhere you look. In the way a baby laughs, the way the human body facilitates breathing and all the million functions that have to work for just one breath to occur. The more you notice perfection, which is divinity embodied, the more you begin to realize that everything is perfection just the way it is. There is a divine genius unfolding, existing, mirroring itself right back at you. Our rigidity, our control, our judgements, our fears begin to soften. You are a perfect divine being. Can you accept that?

Yes, even your pitiful attempt at making pie from scratch when you were feeling ambitious and inspired by that baking show you saw on Netflix (they make it seem so damn easy), that pie is perfect. It is as it should ever be. It's perfect because it taught you how to make a better pie next time, maybe or to find another hobby. It's perfect in the purpose it served for your growth. There is a radical acceptance that comes from within when we are in full alignment with our divinity. We resist nothing. Everything softens. And your gaze upon everything and everyone, including and most importantly your inner-gaze becomes the eyes of God reveling in the perfection of everything co-created into existence. Everything is perfect because everything is divine and touched by the divine. Ever hear the term, "game recognizes game"? God recognizes God. What is Divine recognizes what is Divine. Perfection recognizes Perfection. Darshan — Vision of the Divine — I can see now why that name came to Guru Kirin to be given to me. It was my calling that I was to grow and evolve into — to encompass the eyes to see the divine perfection and genius in everyone and everything, first starting within myself.

This God realization within ourselves, looking through the eyes of the divine externally and most importantly internally completely loosens this tight grip we can develop when we succumb to fear and start to believe we are anything less than divine.

Perfection combined with fear stops us from expressing our authenticity. It stops us from divine play. It stops us from divine creativity. And therefore it stops us from serving and sharing love and our gifts with one another. How tragic of a consequence from this false belief. It's a total work in progress for me, every moment, to be able to have an intimate appreciation of liberated divine perfection and a discernment toward perfection combined with fear that threatens to strangle my playful, divine creativity. Start working on this now, if you haven't already, as this is a big potential sabotage that can derail you or worse, stop you from even beginning.

The Liberation of Vulnerability

"Owning our story can be hard but not nearly as difficult as spending our lives running from it. Embracing our vulnerabilities is risky but not nearly as dangerous as giving up on love and belonging and joy — the experiences that make us the most vulnerable. Only when we are brave enough to explore the darkness will we discover the infinite power of our light. I now see how owning our story and loving ourselves through that process is the bravest thing that we will ever do."

~ *Brené Brown* ~

I really should just refer you to all of Brené Brown's books: *I Thought It Was Just Me (But It Isn't), Rising Strong, The Power of Vulnerability, The Gift of Imperfection, Daring Greatly, Dare to Lead* and her Netflix Special *The Call to Courage.* They are all essentially about the authentic power and liberation in vulnerability. Everything I've learned about vulnerability in my years of creating this healing retreat comes from Brené Brown and my three dogs. My little pack of weirdos all teach me about vulnerability in their own unique ways.

Let's begin with Kalani. My Ewok husky corgi, Kalani. He is the baby of the pack we have here at the healing center. He is very much a healing practitioner and we often refer to him as the Buddha. We don't believe he's a real dog. Evidence shows that he doesn't eat much although he is able to keep his chubby corgi physique. But the fact that he is not food motivated at all truly warms our hearts. Unlike our other animals, we feel he must really love us beyond the sustenance and nourishment we offer him. Kalani also never reacts to things. He's so peaceful and Zen. You only hear his baritone husky howl when he really wants you to pay attention to the energy of what's going on in subtle levels or if he wants you to turn around and reenact the *Dirty Dancing* last scene where Baby runs toward Patrick Swayze and does that swan leap into his arms. Kalani loves to be Baby and run across the field into our arms, flying into a cuddle puddle and belly rub session. He loves the dramatic turn, eye lock, and run. It's pretty adorable. The way Kalani teaches me about vulnerability is how he asks for what he needs without fear of rejection. He wants the *Dirty Dancing* scene over and over again; he will ask for it. He doesn't care if we're too busy, he'll howl ask and what's wonderful about his ask is if you don't indulge him, he's cool with that too and runs to you anyways to give you love.

Rosie, our Australian shepherd queen bee, was given to us by a breeder from the Kohala Coast who wanted Rosie to have a better life and receive more attention. She hoped she would fare well at a retreat center. When she first was handed off to me on the side of a highway, she was covered in mud, and very scared and nervous. Once we got back home from this three-hour drive, I opened the back door and she wouldn't budge and come out. I kept trying to tempt her out with some treats and my high-pitched cajoling and when that didn't work, I tried to physically pull her out and she refused. I was getting impatient with how scared she was. And the minute I turned my attention away, she jumped out and ran into the woods and never came back. I was devastated. We looked everywhere for her that day into the night.

Upon researching Australian shepherds that evening I read in an article that often times, an Australian shepherd is so loyal to one master, that she will traverse an entire countryside to find her master again. I just imagined her starting an epic trek back to Kohala around the entire northern half of the island. I admired her loyalty and felt so bad about my lack of empathy toward her nervousness and grief that afternoon. We put signs up in Volcano and I was called several times that week by neighbors who spotted her by this pond down the road. Every day I would drive by between errands, I would see her, but the moment I stopped and called her name, she ran. I had to be more strategic with my approach. So I started to drive around with a Ziploc bag of shredded kalua pig with me at all times. When I spotted her again at sundown, I parked the car and walked toward her backwards (as I also read to turn your back on dogs so they are not scared and less likely to run away).

I sat down slowly, threw handfuls of kalua pig over my shoulder, and peeked to see if she would eat it. She must have been so hungry as she devoured it. I stayed out there for hours and was ready to just camp out, winning her trust. I ran out of kalua pig though and I was getting super cold and achy so I decided to just drive home and visit her again the next day with more Ziplocs of shredded pork. To my surprise, I saw her slowly following me. I drove five miles per hour back home and when I got out of the truck she was by my door. I put the leash on her but she refused to budge and walk any closer to the house. So, once again, we sat this time under a cypress tree, under the stars and we talked. We made a pact that I would be way more sensitive to her fears, anxiety, and grief if she would start to open her heart and trust me. She started to walk toward the house and she even let me give her a nice bath that night. Rosie taught me about trust, honoring fear, and taking my time with myself and others when fear pops up and feeling safe enough to be vulnerable again.

Then we have our little guy, Oli. He's the oldest now at nine years old. He's a Chihuahua retriever mix. He looks like a mini-golden retriever. He's hairy and stunted and adorable, too. The Chihuahua in him makes him a protective little Napoleon complex fierce beast. He's drawn blood from many with his little nips and he always distrusted humans. A psychic friend once told us that Oli's "past life" was a lion who was shot between his eyebrows by poachers after they had shot the rest of his family. He did have lion-like characteristic. He sat like a lion and acted like he was the king of the jungle. And he licks himself regally like a giant cat too.

Oli teaches me about vulnerability every day. Because even though his first response to most people is to show how tough he is, when people figure out his M.O., and they just sit down and show themselves as non-threatening, and they acknowledge his fierce lion spirit inside his little hairy Chihuahua body, he walks right up to them and shoves his face into any crevice he can find. It's the most tender thing in the Universe.

These dogs are reflections of all aspects of me that I would say are my biggest fears around vulnerability — fear of rejection, needing to feel safe and seen, and feeling like I have to shoulder big responsibilities and must show how tough and strong I am. These fears and false beliefs challenge me to be my most vulnerable and authentic self. Vulnerability is a courageous act of allowing ourselves, our biggest insecurities, longings and fears to be seen no matter what. When we are seen and loved, we soften into vulnerability even more. When others respond with compassion and support when we ask for help, we build up the courage to keep asking for help when we need it. It takes two for vulnerability to work. It takes one to see it and respond to it with gentleness, understanding, compassion and respect and it takes the other to bravely and authentically lean in and show it and let all of ourselves to be seen.

This too is powerful work that I believe will eventually lead to World Peace. As healers, artists, leaders, revolutionaries and change makers — we are not only finding ourselves seated at the proverbial table, but we have to be willing to show up with our weapons down, armors off, and the willingness to be vulnerable and authentic. In fact, it helps us build our own tables in this open-hearted, authentic way, inviting others to show up in their fullness and wholeness, every part of them. I believe this is the greatest Jedi Super Power we can have in these times. We must soften as a human race and allow our full selves to be seen and compassionately be able to see others with radical acceptance and non-judgement — for us to be able to authentically experience Oneness and heal the duality of this breaking world.

Embrace All the Feels (There's a Breakthrough Waiting on the Other Side)

Embracing all of our feelings that come up in challenging moments is part of illuminating our shadows. When we give the stage and shine the spotlight on every single feeling and thought that surfaces we begin the process of learning deeply what our feelings are trying to teach us. There is a wisdom in each feeling and thought on stage. If we were to throw tomatoes at it with our own self-judgments and heckle it with insults and vulgarities, we will lose a beautiful opportunity to listen and understand ourselves and each other better.

Strong feelings especially those of anger and grief, debilitating thoughts, and stern beliefs and observations are incredible fuel for transformation and change. On this land of lava and living between two volcanos, I would say anger is an emotion that is often my personal catalyst for transformation. In the last five years of building and running this healing center, I was given plenty of opportunities to be triggered, so once and for all I can begin to look at anger and its origins for me — my ancestral, historical, parental, societal, political connections and root — so I can heal, evolve and understand myself so much better. I learned how to communicate directly and clearly with minimal charge (an ongoing practice every day) and I learned how to use the fuel of anger to catalyze transformation and alignment in our business and in the people we served and also worked with. I kept receiving reflection after reflection until I was willing enough to really use each instance as an opportunity to get really intimate with anger and hang out with her under the spotlight. I learned a lot. I learned that anger needs to be expressed in the moment and allowed to flow.

Just like the volcano. She vents out of every crack necessary. I learned how to better express anger in the moment without creating more pain in the situation or toward others. I learned to see anger as an opportunity to learn about my unhealed triggers and wounds. I learned the sacredness of anger. The way lava is sacred in its transformative energy. I learned that anger catalyzes us to create clear boundaries. I learned that anger is not toxic, but the suppression, denial, and eventual violent eruption of anger is toxic. I learned that often when anger is ignored and swallowed, it goes to our livers and then eventually our lungs. It can turn into deep melancholy if not allowed its time on stage. What was my kryptonite became my greatest tool especially in communication and catalyzing transformation. Anger can create amazing transformations if you let it and know how to use it as magic.

The Pixar movie *Inside Out* is such an enlightened movie for children that humorously and intelligently addresses how emotions, memories and dreams work and the importance of each emotion within each of us. Not one is better than the other. Certain ones (like sadness) get such a stigma that we often tend to ignore it because it makes us feel uncomfortable. Yet if we learn to embrace them, there is a gem they hold for us in our self-realization, liberation, and continued evolution.

Don't miss the opportunity to receive those gems. Get closer to the fire. There will be a greater chance to transmute these emotions from the pit of your guts and solar plexus where we normally store these emotions up to our hearts and our throats, so that they can be released in effective ways that create positive change in our realities and lives. Being comfortable is not only overrated but extremely boring anyways. We vied for this opportunity to be human and experience all the feels of this existence so we can grow and expand. There are incredible breakthroughs through the uncomfortable moments. Stay in them and stay open.

Healer, Know Thyself

"The closer you come to knowing that you alone create the world of your experience, the more vital it becomes for you to discover just who is doing the creating."
~ Eric Micha'el Leventhal ~

All of this shadow work, which is undeniably difficult and raw but most definitely the most courageous and effective work we humans can do for global peace and planetary transformation, leads to self-realization. "Healer, know thyself" was a phrase my healing arts school teacher, Danilo Retuta, said every day during my apprenticeship with him in his school in Crestone, Colorado. He spent the first half of our curriculum teaching us Qi Gong, the Enneagram, Kundalini Yoga and Meditation, *The Work* by Byron Katie, bringing us to Tibetan empowerments and Blackfoot sweat lodges, and many more self-realization schools of thought and practices so that we can cultivate the deepest most intimate relationship with ourselves first before we even begin to learn about healing modalities and sharing it with others. It was a brilliant curriculum that greatly influences the Luminary's Journey and our Luminaries in Residence Program. I believe it helped me be a much more grounded healing practitioner.

Self-realization must come first — knowing your triggers, knowing your wounds, knowing your shadows. You will be humbled to see all of your reflections — the shadow and the light, your wounds and your genius — as reflections in all of the people you serve. In fact, the more lucid you are and self-aware, the more effective you will be as a healer. You will be a crystal-clear mirror and potent frequency carrier that will be able to recognize the reflections in others and transmute their disharmonies with your awareness, forgiveness, radical acceptance, and love. Your self-awareness holds a tender and safe space for the disharmony of your clients to realign itself into the harmonic frequencies you carry.

This too is Jedi work — it is how the living avatars, like Paramahansa Yogananda and Jesus — healed others. Their self-realization was able to harmonize with any frequency around them because they knew what each frequency was as they embraced it within themselves. We have the ability to be living, breathing, walking, human bioenergetic resonance machines, that can harmonize with every frequency on the planet. The first step in that is to be able to recognize and feel every part of who we are, the shadow and the light. Once we do that and can love, accept and see each part as divinely perfect, we will be able to be in resonance with what is ailing others and transcend that resonance into harmony and balance. Once I realized this through working with bioenergetics quantum healing, I developed a confidence and knowingness that everything disharmonic in our earthly experience can be healed and harmonized. Everything is frequency, after all. Everything is divine. Everything therefore knows its divine nature and resonance.

The more we awaken to our divine nature — all of it — the more we will be able to literally harmonize and heal anything on the spot. I see this happening in my lifetime, which is if I'm blessed, will be fifty years or more on this planet. I just know this in my heart.

8: NOW LEAP OFF THE CLIFF (AND BUILD YOUR WINGS ON THE WAY DOWN)

"It's the possibility of having a dream come true that makes life interesting."
— *Paulo Coehlo*

"Create the highest, grandest vision possible for your life, because you become what you believe."
— *Oprah Winfrey*

Your Vision Board Is Not a Business Plan

If you want to create a healing center and business, even if you're independently wealthy and will be funding it on your own, a solid business plan is key. If you are looking for business partners, investors and/or loans, you will need to get very clear about your numbers and the financial bottom lines. The spiritual, healing and transformative structure is *solid*. The intentions are *solid*. All the amazing quotes from mentors and sages and all of the visions you have of how it will feel and flow is *solid*. That's the *essence* of the business plan that you've been working on throughout this entire Luminary Journey so far and it should feel so very solid to you. You can recite it while you sleep or at family gatherings when you are put on the spot and asked what you're up to. Now, dear Luminary, it's time to look at the *numbers*.

I knew I was in for a ride when I first met Innar. I picked him up on Kalakaua Boulevard in Waikiki. This was almost a decade ago. He was introduced to me by an Estonian healer because he was looking to partner up with someone to create a retreat center in Hawai'i. She had known it was a dream of mine, as I always talked about it with everyone I knew. When I first saw him waiting for me on the corner all of my expectations of what this person could possibly look like just flew out the window. He was dressed head to toe like a fashion model straight out of a Versace advertisement. Tight white pants, pointed leather shoes, a tight cashmere sweater hugging his built frame, sunglasses wrapping around half of his head and a haircut I equated for 1980s Germany for some reason, shaved all around except the top flap of brown hair angling to cover his right eye. "Huh," I thought, "not what I expected at all."

I expected someone to dress more natural and summery, I suppose. He's definitely a different kind of European, I realized. He got into my car and I drove him to the top of Tantalus where I was renting a room in a home built with lava rock at the edge of a cliff. We were going to chat about our individual ideas and visions. We were just getting out of the car and he said, "You don't look like a person with a lot of money."

To my surprise, I realized:

1. This European has judged me as much as I judged him at first sight

2. He has absolutely no social filter from brain to mouth — I loved it and also feared it. (What else is this guy going to say today?)

The truth is, he was right. After spending all my savings in the last four years as I stopped working my nine-to-five and embarked upon my spiritual investigation of life and self, I was starting from scratch again. My bank account had definitely felt the effects of teaching yoga for papayas and art for a couple of years and traveling to wherever Spirit led me to meet my next teachers and go through my next initiations. I was getting my PhD in How to Be a Spirit Living a Human Life. And there are no student loans for this kind of school. As I continued to strip away old identities and travel lighter, I gave away everything when I moved to Hawai'i. My collection of books, jackets, shoes, purses ... everything. All I needed in those years were a few kaftans, slippers and a bathing suit. I was spiritually wealthy. I was joyful, free and fulfilled for the first time in my life. My dwindling savings didn't alarm me at all. I knew I could hustle. I knew I could make money again. It was a matter how I would want to in alignment to who I have discovered I am.

I moved to O'ahu because my soul needed to come back to the world. It was time for me to practice what I've learned. I needed to reconcile with the part of the world I considered to be a matrix and highly illusionary. I needed to heal my relationship with money. I had to get to know money again with this new spiritual framework that has been built inside of me in the last four years. Innar met me at this stage in my life. And I knew, deep down, as I spotted him on Kalakaua Boulevard, in his cashmere and pointed leather shoes, dripping with European swag, that in fact this was my next teacher. What an introduction it was.

"Why do you say that?" I asked nervously, thinking my ego is about to get obliterated right now.

"Oh, I don't know, I just know these things," he said, gently, with a smile on his face as he strolled toward the edge of the cliff overlooking Mānoa Valley.

"Game on," I thought. "Game on, Universe."

Innar was so confident and embodied in his world of money, business, and luxury. And I was so confident in mine of Spirit, transformation and healing. We were both incredible teachers for one another. Two unlikely peas in a pod.

As we got to know each other I gathered that Innar is Batman. His story that is. It is an archetypal Batman story. He lost his parents in a tragic car accident that he was also in but uninjured. They were a very wealthy family in Estonia. And therefore this only child inherited a fortune. He was handsome, charming, intelligent, funny, and exuded a brutal honesty that is so rare in the normal world. I could tell he was also bored and loved to question everything because of his boredom. He even questioned me whenever I said the word "love."

He once said, "When you say you love this and love that, it seems like you love everything, you are diluting the word 'love' to a point that it means nothing." He's a riot. We would get into the most in-depth conversations about love, quantum healing, serving the world. Although we didn't end up working together in creating a retreat center, we've become friends and remained pen-pals to this day. I've witnessed him soften and even say the word "love" more and create snow angels in the mountains of Estonia with his daughters. And he's witnessed me have a much healthier relationship with money and be the boss babe he knew I could be.

What I learned from Innar was how to create a solid business plan. I still laugh to this day at the moment I showed him my "business plan." It was a beyooootiful business plan. It was in green and purple ink. It had inspiring photos of children blowing dandelions in fields of rolling hills and elders reaching out their stunningly beautiful aged hands to the camera. It was moving. It had incredible quotes from visionaries about creating a new world and paragraphs describing intentions and the ideas of what will go into this retreat center. He flipped through the pages and looked up and said, "This isn't a business plan, this is a picture book." Reality check 1,089,652. "Oh, dear Universe," I thought, "thank you for sending me this hilarious teacher from Europe and making this chapter in my life a very interesting adventure."

It can be intimidating to put together a business plan. It can be scary to use a language that you may have never used before. This is the opportunity to literally bridge heaven on earth, marrying together spirit and material. Both are simply energies and when combined together create a very solid and potent contribution to the world that will change lives. I will invoke Innar for you through this process. It won't be as painful and daunting as it feels. And it may even surprise you and you'll realize what a natural you are at it.

Genie in the Bottle

It's time to take your calculators out, turn on your computers, and get an excel sheet or your notebook opened. It's time to get cracking on some lists. It will be elevating to bring together all of the moving parts in creating this healing center and also very ground-ing when you learn of all of the costs.

What you will first want to do mentally, emotionally and ener-getically is imagine that a genie has come out of your teapot, and is now asking you to just start writing down your dream list. This is *everything* and *anything* you are seeing when you time travel and visit your healing center when it has opened its doors and provid-ing exceptional service to your clients. Go there, explore each room and detail and start free writing it all down in your notebook or computer screen. Open up the files or photo albums where you gathered inspiration in the past and let those images/references spark even more details to add to this list.

This is again, a very elevating exercise and allow yourself to be taken into these realms. What will you create if you knew you will be supported? This is the questions you write on top of this list and go for it, have fun.

When you are done, it's time to categorize your list. I suggest the following categories to be:

- Real Estate
- Construction/Building
- Interior Design
- Healing Services & Material
- Administrative
- Marketing/Publicity
- Staff
- Miscellaneous (Farming, Apothecary, Animals etc.)

Take your dream list that you've compiled and place each item on that list under one of these categories. How does that start to feel? Take this moment and just sit with this list and these categories and allow this organizing energy to integrate within you. This is an incredible milestone to see what has been in your vision and heart, manifest itself into an organized list in front of you. Wonderful job!

Now roll up your sleeves and it's time to do research on the range of costs for everything on this list. Research can mean looking each item up on Google or calling around and asking quotes from vendors, contractors, designers, web developers, marketers, colleagues and friends. You are finding the energetic and monetary value for each material and service you have envisioned as the bones and structure of your healing center.

Here's an incredible tip that I learned through trial and error: get the full spectrum range of what something will cost. Don't immediately just look at what would be the least expensive. Familiarize yourself with the range of costs and know the spectrum of quality. No matter what kind of budget you have or believe you can manifest, you will want to choose the numbers that are mid-range to the highest when you create your business plan. Yet at the same time knowing the lower end costs too. When you are actually building and creating your center, aligning yourself to the mid-range to highest range quality materials and services is the long term level of quality you want as a foundation in creating your center and you will also know (if/when you have to) the lower end costs of materials and services you may need to use as the budgets and circumstances may fluctuate and ask of you to be flexible. Doing this now, will save you plenty of time in the future. Having this clarity now also, will give you the appreciation for the higher quality materials and services and the drive to manifest the resources to stay in that range of high quality through the creation process of your center.

This process can take some time. But remember, once you put words and numbers to your vision – this act of "spelling" and infusing magic into these words and numbers, will accelerate the magnetism of the resources needed to bring your visions into reality. As Paulo Coelho writes, "when you want something, all the Universe conspires in helping you achieve it." You will notice the momentum you have created and how suddenly the information you are seeking, the materials and services you have been researching will start to pop up in your waking daily life seemingly out of nowhere. Enjoy these synchronicities and ease. Recognize each one and express gratitude for each one, and God will continue to bring you more and more of these insights and alignments. I've come to realize that God *loves* to co-create with us in this way. She *loves* it when we invoke our magic and embody it into tangible realities. It's God's favorite game and pastime – creation. Enjoy this part of this process. It's teaching you just how supported you are and will continue to be.

The Blueprint

I thank my mom and dad for conceiving me when they did so I can come to this Earth as a Virgo (in Gregorian Astrology) and a Leo (in Vedic Astrology). I'll take both sun signs and cosmically innate superpowers. My astrological alignment makes me a prime creator of business plans I realized. I love to organize visions into blueprints. It's my zone of genius (as Gay Hendricks calls it) and I didn't even know that until I tried doing it. Innar was my fairy godfather who tapped my head with his wand (of brutal honesty) and helped me remember. No matter what astrological sign you are though, it is your divine nature and super power to create order from chaos. Yes, no matter how allergic you feel to such things. I have found that the more I recognize this Divine Intelligence birthing through me, the more I want my affairs, my space, my creations to be organized and harmonic.

Your experience in school, maybe math class, could have convinced you otherwise, but that is a program we can easily reboot, rewire, and renew. I had a friend who told me that she would literally get very sleepy and often fall asleep whenever numbers, calculations, taxes, bills were the tasks at hand in front of her. It perplexed her and she didn't care to explore why as she just accepted this odd fact about herself and let her accountant mother deal with all things regarding numbers. She had number-induced narcolepsy, was my amateur diagnosis. It was so fascinating to me that I offered to explore that with her if she wanted. Why not? I mean, maybe we'll discover that she's been hypnotized once and she forgot but the spell was, anytime numbers came up, she would just fall asleep right then and there … in front of the bank teller, in front of an ATM, when she picked up her mail and saw it was a bill. "I mean, this could be so dangerous," I joked.

We traced it back to fifth grade and doing math homework during a really stressful time in her family's life. Her parents were on their way to divorce and she was absorbing a lot of the fighting (which happened to be around finances) and she was emotionally exhausted. Her go-to was sleep. She also couldn't figure out the math problems but had no one to help her at home, or at least she felt she couldn't bother anyone to ask. This memory and emotional coping mechanism was up for a reboot, rewire, and renew.

We can always track our resistances and limiting beliefs. Remember – you were born with divine gifts of manifestation. You can create realities with your thoughts and intentions. So it's a matter of clearing any (mental, emotional, and energetic) calcified scar tissue from injuries you've absorbed in your life that covers and buries these divine gifts you were born with. Your Human Blueprint is a replica of the Divine Blueprint. This Healing Center Blueprint is a replica of God's Earth Blueprint. It is genius, it is the perfect alchemy of spirit and material. Know that, and let's begin.

Here is the structure to follow for your blueprint/business plan:

1. Cover

2. Index

3. Opening Letter to Who You're Presenting It To

4. The Big Picture / Vision / What It is You are Creating

5. Your Team and Bios/Credentials (including yourself and if it's only you, then write about you and refer to the different roles you are looking to fill)

6. The Structure and Design of the Physical Space and Working Infrastructure

7. The Detailed Line Item Costs of the Structure, Design, Administrative, Marketing, Day to Day Up and Running Costs

8. The Services / Programs / Offerings of the Healing Center

9. The Line Item Fees You Will Charge and Total Income You Expect (5 Year Growth Plan)

10. Your Proposal and Pitch for Loan/Investment You Need and its Allocation During Building Process (timing and amount needed per phase)

11. The Return on Investment / Loan Payback You Project (amount and time) and Any Extra Perks/Bonuses

12. The Wrap Up – Restate the Vision, How It Will Benefit the Community Locally and Globally, and a Short and Sweet Thank You (include your contact info)

These are the bare bones of a business plan. As Innar taught me, a potential investor will breeze through the first ten sections and will look for The Return on Investment page. I didn't find that true in my case, but I appreciated what he was trying to prepare me for and teach me. The numbers matter. The bottom lines matter to investors and loan offices. Even if they are your family, friends, patrons, and biggest supporters. Now with that said, do not hold back in also infusing your business plan with prayer, your intentions, your multi-dimensional vision. When that is married to the numbers, you've got yourself a Divine Blueprint. Bring on heaven on earth, baby! You're on your way.

Calling All Angels (Investors, Business Partners, Loans and Crowdfunding Campaigns)

It's time to start a new list. Categorize it as so:

• Investors

• Business Partners

• Loans/Grants (Bank, Organizations & Private)

• Crowdfunding Campaigns

And scan your mental and physical rolodex to see who your supporters and partners in this creation will be. This will entail scanning your life. The friends, family friends, and communities you've been a part of. The schools, universities and organizations you have been a part of. The programs, workshops, celebrations, and movements you have been a part of. These are all relevant places where divine appointments have occurred in your life. Most often, these are the people who will help you or network you to find the alignment you are looking for. You will need to research loans (banks and private loans and grants) and also the best crowd-funding campaigns that have been successfully used by people you have seen creating similar centers and offerings as you.

Before I begin to scan my life and tune into people and organizations, I like to get into a zone of meditation to open myself up to the clearest and highest alignment. Since Kundalini Yoga and Meditation is my background, I love using the Sobagh Kriya as my way of tuning in to this realm as it is a Kriya and technology that specifically draws in money and abundance. The very first time I did this Kriya in my twenties fresh out of Kundalini yoga teacher training, I applied for jobs that same day and I received three out of the four that I applied to that day. I didn't need any more convincing that this Kriya works. If you resonate with this Kriya, I would highly recommend practicing it for forty days – the days it will take to rewire old habits and create new ones.

Kundalini Kriyas are one of the most advanced practices and tools I have in my medicine magic box. If this is your first time practicing Kundalini yoga and meditation, I suggest finding a teacher or class in your community and specifically ask a teacher to lead you through this Kriya so you can see it demonstrated properly.

If you can't find one in your community, there is always good old YouTube. They have several recordings of teachers demonstrating this specific Kriya. If you have other practices that resonate with you, with your spiritual and/or ancestral lineage, I would begin a practice today with this manifestation in mind. It is time to take all of these big visions and funnel it into a focused and potent force of energy. These are Jedi Super Powers at its core.

Yogi Bhajan Teaches Sobagh Kriya: Invoke the Wealth of the Universe
(Taught by Yogi Bhajan on 6/21/96 at Summer Solstice)

Your normal process of life is to not give; not giving yourself a chance, not giving to others. You do not believe in creating a vacuum. When there is a vacuum, God must fill it. I'm not saying that you are poor. But you could have more. Giving is the way of the rich – giving services, giving expertise, giving work, giving to others to get blessings, giving something for prayer, giving to the needy.

You don't pay attention. You sometimes just don't want to do anything. Sometimes you are not very agreeable. You are more concerned with scare tactics, with insecurities, than with your power to expand. I'm trying to give you a very handy tool so that you can be anywhere, and you can become rich. I'm not going to give you printed money, but I'm giving you a tool of prosperity. Will that be cool? All right, let's do it.

And I'd like you to be your own judge. See how it works. There are a lot of things that you think you can't do, like looking unique or being excellent. But you only think these things because you are afraid of the responsibility. If the psyche is corrected once in a while, for a few minutes here, or a few minutes there, you'll be surprised how much good you can do for yourself.

This is a five-part kriya. Each part must be practiced for an equal amount of time, either 3 minutes or 11 minutes. Do not exceed 11 minutes. Only Meditation #1 can be practiced on its own, separately from the other exercises.

Meditation #1

To become rich and prosperous with wealth and values is to have the strength to come through. It means transmissions from your brain and the power of your intuition can immediately tell you what to do. By practicing this meditation, you will be in a position to immediately change gears. If you need to go in reverse, you can go in reverse. If you need to go forward, you can go forward.

This is a very simple, old system. This is called "moon mound." (Indicates outer side of hand along the small finger.) This side of my hand along the index finger is called Jupiter. Put the thumbs under the index fingers. (Thumbs cross below the hands, with the right thumb under the left.) I hit the Moon; I hit Jupiter. You are thinking, "What is this going to do?" This is going to straighten your head out.

Chant with Tantric *Har* with each movement. Alternate hitting the moon sides and the Jupiter sides of the hands together at the level of the heart center. Eyes should be nine-tenths dosed, focusing on the tip of the nose. You should not do it for more than three minutes when you are working during the daytime or you'll become too rich! No, no, I'm not kidding with you. Hey, you guys, you think I am joking. Come on; let's do what works.

You are not going to mint all the money right now, but this is what I am telling you. Any time when you are puzzled and you are in bad shape, do three minutes of this meditation. If you do it for eleven minutes a day, it's more than enough. Doing too much will be greed. It stimulates the mind: the Moon center and the Jupiter. When Jupiter and the Moon come together, there is no way in the world you will not create wealth. I'm not talking of money. Money is a common word. Money is only a medium. I'm talking of wealth. It'll come to you.

What I'm trying to tell you is that it's all in you. It's not outside. Just stimulate certain parts of the brain. I'm not going to do anything. It's going to work

Meditation #2

Now, there are times when you are depressed, there are times you are impressed. When you are impressed, you usually do the wrong things. Are you listening? And when you are depressed, you always do wrong things. That's a fact. When you are impressed, you don't use your intuition.

Stretch your arms up sixty degrees. Open your fingers, spreading them widely. The fingers have to be totally hard. If you do it correctly, you will get the results. I will only tell you. I'm not going to do it for you. Look at how hard my fingers are. They are open. Now, in rhythm with the same Tantric *Har* tape but without chanting out loud, cross your arms alternating right over left and then left over right, still keeping the fingers stretched open.

Right in front, left behind. Fingers spread wide, arms open. Left in front, right behind.

Meditation #3

Now this is an English mantra. Watch. You know this id, the thumb? Put them both in your fists and press as hard as you can, like you are going to squeeze the blood out of them. Press, press, press hard. Arms at sixty degrees.

Move the arms in small backward circles. Press the id. Press, press, press hard. With each circle you make of your arms chant "God." Chant "God" powerfully from the navel. Come on, machos. You are getting out of shape. From the navel. Okay, okay, that's it.

The word "God" has three letters: "G," which generates; "O," which organizes; and "D," which delivers and destroys. They are three sounds: G-O-D. God. When "God" is chanted from here (points to his navel point), then God can hear. When you chant "God" from the mouth, it makes no difference. He doesn't even hear it. For this meditation it can only be chanted when you take the id and squeeze it really hard. And the circle has to be powerful. The entire spine shakes. Sometimes you'll find you are lifting yourself from the ground. Don't worry. It's not a small exercise. Now keep it going: stretch it, tight, tight, as tight as you can. And the circle should be tight.

Meditation #4

All right, relax. Suppose nothing works in your life – you don't remember things, you want to get out of trouble, but you can't reach anybody. (Yogi Bhajan demonstrates the posture and mantra. The right hand goes up and the left hand goes down; palms facing the body; hand cross each other.)

Har Haray Haree, Wahe Guru. The mantra is a sound current through the tongue and upper palate. *Har Haray Haree, Wahe*

Guru (*Wahe* is pronounced "wa-hay"). Continue chanting in a low monotone. Like Tibetans. Keep going. Deeper – from the base. Cut down your karmas forever. Deeper sound from the navel. Try it with honesty. Don't slack off. (Six minutes .) Now whisper. Strongly whisper. Use the prana (breath). Burn any disease. Change the metabolism. (Three minutes.) Whistle. (Two minutes.) Then stop it. (If you are doing this meditation for three minutes total, each part is done for one minute.)

Meditation #5

Put your arms at shoulder level, left hand under, right over. Breathe long and deep. Don't let the hands fall. They should be parallel to the ground; that's the law.

Keep your spine straight; sit correctly. Do nothing; just breathe one breath a minute: 20 seconds to inhale, 20 seconds to hold, 20 seconds to exhale. Try it. See what it does for you. Breathe consciously one breath a minute.

This is a complete set. It is called Sobagh Kriya.

If there is a misfortune written by the will of God, by doing this set you will make it into good fortune. I'm not saying "man-made." I'm saying if God Himself has written that you shall live under misfortune, by doing Sobagh Kriya you can turn your misfortune into prosperity, good fortune, and good luck.

This is the most sacred and absolutely most powerful kriya of Kundalini Yoga. And it is in parts. You can do each part either 3 minutes or 11 minutes, not more. If you do 3 minutes, do 3 minutes, 3 minutes, 3 minutes, 3 minutes, and 3 minutes. If you do 11 minutes, do 11, 11, 11, 11, 11. That's the time. And do not exceed.

I repeat, do not exceed. So, I'd advise you to move very cautiously, very slowly. Affectionately practice it.

© *The Teachings of Yogi Bhajan*

Even if you didn't stop and actually practice this particular Kriya, do take a few deep breaths and center yourself in the way you know how. Connect to the deep center of the earth and open your crown to connect to the energies of the heavens. Ask your Higher Self to tune into the human angels and enlightened organization on Earth who would be the most graceful, joyful, and mutually beneficial (big win-big win) partners for you in this endeavor. And also ask your Higher Self the *qualities* of these human angels and organizations that would be the most harmonic for you to co-create this healing center with. Imagine that you are putting this signal out from your very attuned broadcasting Spirit Antenna out into the Universe (because you are). Sit and simply be open and see whose faces, names, qualities, and/or energy come to your mind and heart. Write them down. Don't think about them. Just enjoy this moment of channeling and being simply an instrument. When you've finished, take a breath, and bless up this list with gratitude for the clarity and the gifts these individuals, institutions, and qualities bring to the world already. And then bow down to yourself in gratitude for being a visionary and broker of these sacred resources which you are about to amplify in energy and circulation for this healing center and the blessings this center will ripple out into the lives of many you will be serving.

The Art of Asking and Receiving

Something what can be intimidating and cause all kinds of paralyzing anxiety within yourself is the exact portal into deep growth and transformation you will take as a spiritual leader of a healing center in the making. Like every fear that is known to mankind, this particular fear of asking for support and receiving support (in whatever form) is rooted in our fear that we are not divine. In more practical words, it is a fear rooted in the belief that we are not worthy. We are not deserving. That this healing center and service to the planet is not worthy or deserving to make the difference it's supposed to make and bless the people it's supposed to bless. Wait, hold up. That last part, does not ring true to you? You know this center is meant to be of service to this world? You know it deserves to be of service to people? You wouldn't be coming this far in creating it. You certainly wouldn't have created a business plan and done all the research and self-work to get to this moment if you didn't think this service wasn't meant to exist in the world. Then where is the fear coming from? What belief can we track it to? It's that calcification of scar tissue again, perhaps this one is around our self-worth. Who are we to ask for this support? Who are we to be trusted with this much support and money? Who are we to be gifted with this divine mission and vision? We can spend the rest of this book, tracking the roots of self-worth. However, let's move through this in one elegantly efficient swoop. Who are we to *not* accept our divine birthright to be vessels of healing and transformation for this planet?

If you have this vision and this desire in your heart to create a healing center that will elevate the lives of many people, you have been given a gift so precious to birth and nurture. You are the divine co-parent of this gift. Who is the other co-parent? God. Straight up God. Talk about a Power House Couple. Jay-Z and Beyoncé. Isis and Osiris. Jesus and Mary Magdalene. These power couples cannot compare to that kind of union you've got going on with God. You and God creating this baby of a vision together – there is no limit when your co-creator is God besides the limitations you may believe you have and manifest yourself. Let us integrate that. It's a big one. Get intimate with God. Get intimate with the divine power within you and this level of co-creation.

One of the greatest lessons I learned through my own pro- cess of aligning to investors, receiving monetary support, loans, investments, gifted resources, and a crowdfunding campaign is this: you are presenting an incredible gift to someone to use their gifts and resources and amplify it more in the world through this service and center you are creating. This is an incredible opportu- nity to amplify *love, healing,* and *transformation.* The living human angels and organizations whom you will ask and are aligned to this co-creation with you will know what an incredible opportunity this is within them. You have a divine appointment and contract to co-create this together. God, your co-creation partner, will send them a memo. Believe and trust that. They will know. Your only responsibility is to share this opportunity with them, with all of your authenticity and vulnerability and the clarity of your vision. This is the alignment within.

If you get a no in whatever form you receive it, it only means that they have other divine appointments that come first. This is not your divine appointment right now. Maybe in another time yes. And I've had that happen to me too. Timing is everything. But you will not know that until you make the offer and appointment. Do not take this no personally and let it discourage you. In fact, celebrate the clarity as you are getting closer to the divine alignment that has already been set before you embarked upon this journey.

When you receive the *yes*, celebrate and then ground. What I mean by ground is take out the tool of discernment and tune into the offer, agreement, investor and organization. Does it still feel like a win-win? Remember this is your baby you are co-creating with God. While being open to the divine alignments you must also be discerning to what is not divinely aligned but can seem like it at first glance. It may be an incredible test in your self-worth. I've had to learn this very important significance the hard way too. And we will discuss it more in detail in the *Soul of Money* section in the next chapter.

Just like the inner-alignment needed for asking, it is the same inner-alignment needed for receiving. The remembrance of your divine co-creation with God is the inner-alignment. The resonance and intention and energy of this opportunity you are offering must harmonically resonate with the giver – in reciprocal directions. It is a mutual resonance. In other words, just because someone is willing to give you what you're asking for, does not mean that you should receive it if there are some non-resonating flags that come up. However, if every single cell within your being says *yessss* and is resonating in the divine-appointment level, then *celebrate* this alignment. Bow down to yourself, give praise to God for sending that memo loud and clear and acknowledge the living human angel(s) and organizations in front of you. You are all entering the next level of amplifying your light and love into the world.

9: ASCENSION BACK TO EARTH

"When you are inspired by some great purpose, some extraordinary project, all your thoughts break their bonds; your mind transcends limitations; your consciousness expands in every direction; and you find yourself in a great, new and wonderful world."
~ Patanjali ~

Kintsugi

When our minds are being seeded with incredible insights and ideas, it can be very intoxicating. Visionaries are perfectly at home in that world. The Great Work we have ahead of us is to anchor all of that back to Earth, into something with structure, essence, and function. We ascend the mountain and reach the peak and we soon understand that is not the pinnacle of our journey. It is the return, the implementation of what we've learned and most importantly the way we shall serve our communities and therefore deepen our experience of our own divine embodiment.

This is where my spiritual life began to get very real in a way that I was given one opportunity after the other to embody the spiritual wisdom I've learned within every moment of my day, week, month and years. It was a full-time enrollment into The Great Mystery School of all Mystery Schools.

Healing Centers are energetic temples that are anchoring in the energies of transformation and light on this planet. That's incredible if you think about it. Imagine the kind of cosmic energy channeling through you and all of the people that take part in creating it with you. The magnitude of it, never really dawned on me in its fullness and depth, until now, when I look back on the journey. So much happened. There was so much karma that played out and cleared. There was so much healing and transformation. There were so many tears, laughter, and awe. There were so many failures and heartbreak and then triumphs too. It was everything.

I remember when we were getting ready to open, I went into a panic. I thought, I can't even imagine opening after all of that. I feel like I'm good. I can close up shop now and feel really accomplished. I could have used an entire year before opening our doors just to integrate the lessons I learned in the creation process. There were times during our building phase where I thought, if I had known it was going to be this challenging, I don't think I would do it.

The process reminds me so much of the Japanese process called Kintsugi, fixing broken pottery with lacquer and powdered gold. It is their process that embraces and treats cracks and brokenness as part of the divine beauty and divine perfection of the object rather than something to be covered up or thrown away. In fact, they believe there is more strength and beauty in the cracks that are now highlighted by gold.

Sharing these lessons, anecdotes, and stories with you is my form of Kintsugi. The queen of vulnerability Brené Brown, in her Netflix special *The Call to Courage*, cites this quote from Theodore Roosevelt as being the quote that ignited her passion to dedicate her research and service in exploring vulnerability and sharing it with the world. This quote is from a speech Roosevelt gave in 1910 at the Sorbonne in Paris, France:

"It is not the critic who counts; not the man who points out how the strong man stumbles, or where the doer of deeds could have done them better. The credit belongs to the man who is actually in the arena, whose face is marred by dust and sweat and blood; who strives valiantly; who errs, who comes short again and again, because there is no effort without error and shortcoming; but who does actually strive to do the deeds; who knows great enthusiasms, the great devotions; who spends himself in a worthy cause; who at the best knows in the end the triumph of high achievement, and who at the worst, if he fails, at least fails while daring greatly, so that his place shall never be with those cold and timid souls who neither know victory nor defeat."

You found this book. You're dreaming of creating a healing center to make a difference in this world. You're about to go all in and dive deep into your embodiment. You have more than earned the right to hear my story. Thank you bearing witness to it. And one day, you will be sharing your journey to other Luminaries seeking your wisdom and medicine.

The Alchemy of Heaven on Earth

I believe healing centers sprouting in every corner of this earth will create heaven on earth. I believe when humans heal and transform remembering they are gods and goddesses living a human existence, we will experience and live heaven on earth. I believe healing centers are modern day temples anchoring in and shining light into the world – as spiritual and energetic light houses. I dedicate the rest of my life to supporting centers to be created like this all over the world. I dedicate my life to creating some of my own too.

I also believe we are walking vibrations of these healing centers as we heal and transform within. So as we gather in transformative retreats and heal vulnerably and create gardens and celebrate our humanity, we are anchoring more and more light into this plane through our embodiment. I believe for Luminaries like ourselves, this is our greatest mission that keeps us up at night, and makes us spring out of bed in the morning. And no matter what is occurring in our lives, no matter what challenges may come, it is the courage of vulnerability that continues to keep us going. We are temple creators, dream weavers, and love alchemists. And we are willing to dig our hands into this earth and embody the qualities of the divine within us more and more each day. I believe this can create the greatest revolution this planet has ever seen.

I believe what the lineage of Sages have said, that we are on the precipice of a Golden Age and what we are in is The Great Shift they have foreseen for centuries. I believe every human has roles they are called to play in this Great Shift. And I believe the time is *now* to activate ourselves and support one another in embodying the roles we were born to embody to get this golden age poppin'. This Great Shift will take all of us working together in authentic and embodied ways. Putting to practice these spiritual values that are based upon unconditional love, radical truth, crystal clarity, and the willingness to serve each other and this planet because we realize we are One – this is what we are being called forward to do. It will take all of what you know and embody within. Because it is about full and authentic embodiment which means being radically honest with ourselves and realizing the only thing stepping in our way of this full embodiment is our own selves. What a fascinating Earth curriculum we've agreed to take part in! The good news is we are destined to succeed because everything we need is already within us and up for our discovery and use.

The Soul of Money

In the last chapter, I spoke of healing my relationship with money. Lynn Twist and her book *The Soul of Money* was one of those books like *The Autobiography of a Yogi* that rearranged my cellular structures and consciousness so much that it also quickly rearranged my reality, almost instantaneously. I give both books away as often as I can, because it was that impactful for me and I trust it may be for others as well, especially for those who come to the retreat with the same questions they are exploring in their lives as I had. Both books have taught me that Spirit and Material are one and the same thing. It is all energy and our relationship to this energy makes all the difference. It can create heaven on earth or hell on earth.

As Paramahansa Yogananda says, "Destroy the false division between material and spiritual work." In the journey to create this healing center, I am finally beginning to understand what he means. Everything we do is sacred. Everything we use is a sacred tool. And that includes money. That was the biggest paradigm shift I had in my relationship with money. To realize that money is sacred and it will allow me to continue to amplify my service to the sacred as I embrace it and value it for its energy and potential to amplify, bless, and love up people, this Earth and the revolutionary movements ushering in a Great Awakening – is everything.

Many of us have been raised with unhealthy and sometimes traumatic relationships with money. It is one of the biggest programs on Earth. The false beliefs of lack, not having enough, having to suffer for it, seeing people suffer because of the imbalance use of it, unjust systemic use of it to perpetuate poverty, hunger, racism, classism and attacks on self-worth – the list is endless. It is our job now to unravel that and heal these traumas to the core. Lifting the illusions projected upon money.

Money, like love, is simply energy. Yes, there are folks that try to hurt each other in the name of "love," but that's not love. Love is a frequency not defined by how people try to manipulate it from their own consciousness of pain and confusion. Money is a frequency not defined by how people try to manipulate it from their own consciousness of pain and confusion. When I understood this and released my programing around it, the energy of money was free and pure in my life. It is as holy as love. It all depends on how you use it. It was liberated from the prison I had it in. I became harmonic with it as my natural birthright. And with any intimate relationship, it's a work in progress. When we hit snags, I use it to examine my internal belief systems and alignment.

Start here. Before you go any further, start here with the intimate relationship you have with money. Examine any beliefs, wounds and trauma you hold that create the story that money is somehow a negative energy that can cause you pain and suffering and perform a psychic surgery on your consciousness around that (gently and with nothing but love and understanding for yourself). How do you do such a psychic surgery? It's flipping the belief and wording you have around money. For example, "money is evil" – "money is energy and when used generously for the good of all, it is divine." Because, like love, money is a frequency. When aligned with service to all that is sacred, it will help usher in heaven on earth. Lynn Twist writes:

> *"The happiest and most joyful people I know are those who express themselves through channeling their resources – money, when they have it – on to their highest commitments. Theirs is a world where the experience of wealth is in sharing what they have, giving, allocating, and expressing themselves authentically with the money they put in flow."*

I believe this to be highest form of wealth on Earth. It is spiritual wealth in which Spirit and material have truly alchemized as one within each of us and we are divinely embodied conduits of its energy.

After you've explored your relationship with money and healed core beliefs and stories that separate you from the frequency of abundance, let's take it to the next level. I learned two huge lessons from Lynn Twist that came up right away as living lessons in the creation of our healing center.

My first paradigm-shifting lesson: when you proclaim what you stand for, there is a vortex of energy that forms in all of Creation that magnetizes all of the support and resources needed (of Spirit and of Matter) to you. She encourages us to see ourselves as needlepoints wherever we are standing and living our lives. And as we strengthen the intention and prayer within every cell of our being, for what we stand for and what we dedicate our gifts and lives to, it becomes a crystal clear frequency that emits out into the Universe. It is felt by everyone and everything, most especially God. "Ah ha," God says, "there she is; let's give her what she needs. She's able to anchor that energy into her body, life and earth." Our task is to stay centered and grounded in what we stand for so we can receive all the blessings showering upon us. We are poised and ready to meet every opportunity, magical synchronicity, and abundant blessing that is funneled to the beam of light we are emitting on this planet.

This goes for your very own being and the healing center you are creating. These are needlepoints of concentrated light piercing into this earth and reaching into the depths of heaven. When I first integrated this, I felt it physically and energetically realign and open up my spine. It was as if I was experiencing a Kundalini Awakening all over again. Within every cell I knew this was truth and I committed myself to living it daily.

My second paradigm shifting lesson from Lynn Twist: The energy in which money is given to you, *matters*. So be discerning. I eluded to this huge lesson in the previous chapter when we were exploring the topic of investors, business partners, and loans. Lynn Twist shares an incredible story of returning her first huge donation to The Hunger Project back to the CEO of a corporation recently accused of poisoning their buyers. The intention in which the money was given didn't feel right to her. It felt like a publicity pay-off and didn't feel authentic. Something about that lesson just sent thunderbolts through my consciousness while I was taking it in. Soon after, I was aligned to another potential investor. He was willing to invest into the project the exact amount I was asking for and praying for. I was so grateful and thought, this is it, it's really happening! I've never even imagined it was going to be that quick. As if it came out of nowhere! It was the most money I have ever seen and I was starry eyed and elated.

As we negotiated the contracts, red flags started to come up. One, he wanted fifty-one percent ownership of the business. Two, he kept telling me I wasn't experienced enough to run a business. Three, he was talking badly about vendors to me and also talking badly about me to vendors, trying to establish his power by creating division amongst us. Four, how he earned his money and the services he provided was actually harming the earth. This one was the biggest one of them all. This may be obvious to you, to not align with these red flags. But for me, there were certain qualities he had that were aligned. And I made those qualities way more important and let them blind me to the shadows and red flags. The amount of money and my longing to create this center made me ignore my gut feelings. This was such a huge lesson for me to integrate how that feels and how convincing myself to ignore signs feels. It's an incredible lesson to learn.

I started to have bad dreams about him and so did my mother. Despite our excitement about the potential of this project moving forward, I had to say no and walk away. I was empowered in my decision because of what I just read from Lynn Twist. I knew that wasn't a coincidence, and I knew there was a reason why I felt thunderbolts when I read it. Trust your instincts. Trust your intuition. Trust how everything feels during the process of money negotiations. Trust the red flags. Do not be blinded by the money and potential because the frequency in how it is made, held and offered matters.

With that said, be a conduit of money in which as it flows through your being you are blessing it up in all directions. That blessing will multiply and amplify your prayers and sacred service and visions. I highly recommend *The Soul of Money*. If you end up visiting me at our healing center, mention this chapter and I'll give you a free copy. (I strive to be a book fairy godmother like Oprah. So, mahalo for the opportunity). I'll end with this beautiful quote from Lynn Twist that encapsulates anything and everything I could possibly say about the magnificent soul of money:

> *"Money is like water. It can be a conduit for commitment, a currency of love. Money moving in the direction of our highest commitments nourishes our world and ourselves. What you appreciate appreciates. When you make a difference with what you have, it expands. Collaboration creates prosperity. True abundance flows from enough; never from more. Money carries our intention. If we use it with integrity, then it carries integrity forward. Know the flow – take responsibility for the way your money moves in the world. Let your soul inform your money and your money express your soul."*

On Design and Building

This is where it gets really fun. I believe there is a genetic code within us all that carries the genius of God's eye for design. We inherently know what feels good, looks good, and functions optimally for what we want to infuse inside of it. Nature is a living, breathing, exalted proof of this. Forests are the first ever cathedrals. Healing centers will function at their best if physically designed in harmony with the spirit of its purpose and offering taking its inspiration from the laws of nature as natural law is harmony embodied. It's like biomimicry – the human made design that mimics the genius of nature. Its functional goal is elegant efficiency. Its aesthetic goal is divine natural beauty. Its spiritual intention is that the space itself creates space for the humans who inhabit it to connect to their divinity, to surrender to their healing, and to be inspired in their transformation and creativity. This goes for homes, schools, business spaces, restaurants, temples – every space where humans gather.

If I could live multiple lives in this moment, I would immerse myself in architecture school. Thank goodness for technology and this movement called EdX. I studied architecture on-line from Harvard professors who put together an amazing curriculum that activates your mind to think like an architect. I highly recommend seeking out this kind of wisdom and downloading it for yourself. It makes talking to architects, contractors and builders so much more empowering. I also studied biomimicry and am fascinated and inspired by architecture that takes the genius of nature and bases its design on its simple yet profound functionality. As we enter the Golden Ages, I believe we will see more and more architectural masterpieces, homes, offices, and centers created in this fashion.

Eugene Tsui was my very first architecture crush. He was an Olympian, clothing designer, and architect – a Renaissance man to the T. He designs his own clothes and he dresses as if you combine Buddhist Monk attire with Star Trek attire. He built his parents a home modelled after a dinosaur. I believe it's in California and it had won the title of the most indestructible home in the United States. His style is Jetsons meets the Flintstones. Monolithic and the space feels like you're inside an animal or plant.

I highly recommend you finding architecture and architectural philosophies that make your heart sing. If you are building and designing structures, this will be an incredible opportunity to tap into the genius of God and truly set some potent intentions in the structure, foundation, intention of these spaces.

The key to this phase is hiring the best team for your vision. The way your team communicates, the way they see the world, the earth, healing and transformation matters. The team I am working with now, impressed me when they asked me these questions, "what is sacred to you and what is a non-negotiable in the building and designing of your center?" I was like, whoa … that's deep. They asked and said the magic words and with their questions, I knew we were the right fit, as we spoke the same language and had similar priorities in design.

Being a woman in this field is a bit challenging too. In our first go-around building this center, I was profiled as a gullible, husband-less, easy to manipulate client. Little did they know, the psychic and intuitive strength I had. Add that to my mercurial disposition, it was such a clash of power, will and egos. If I could do it over again, I would have hired a project manager immediately. For two years, I project managed our first build-out and it was torture. A huge learning curve for me on how to hold my ground, how to see the red flags from contractors out to just rip you off, how to negotiate prices, how to draw contracts on payments and timing. The Spirit and the Material once again – another incredible opportunity to learn how to alchemize these energies in this process of design and building.

I learned so much through this process. I became one of the most beloved customers at Home Depot, sans some of my meltdowns. I always made it up by bringing some burritos over to the contractors station where I spent 50 percent of my time. I was the errand girl and the negotiator. I was the boss and the chef. I dove into the deep end without even knowing it and I learned to swim. Now, in my second go around in designing and building for our expansion, I feel so equipped and ready to practice all of the lessons I have learned and then some. I'm excited to work with a project manager, an architect, a structural engineer, a community design expert, an interior designer – a team I've recently curated knowing what I know now.

On Multi-Dimensional Tasking

As an entrepreneur, my first year was wearing every single hat and playing every single role in creating and running this healing retreat and just winging it. I vacuumed and did laundry, I thought of marketing and advertised retreats, I massaged the clients, I performed bioenergetics medicine, I did the grocery shopping for retreats, I represented myself in court for folks I had to sue, I did our bookkeeping, I interviewed and hired our independent contractors, I ran our social media campaigns, I cooked and sous-cheffed for our visiting chefs, I repaired small things, I tiled floors, I planted our veggies and fruit trees, I was a therapist and sometimes dysfunctionally the mother for many temporary staff, I made beds and learned the hotel folds, I booked and scheduled retreats, I made posters ... you get the drift? They say, entrepreneurs leave 40/hour-a-week-soul-sucking jobs with steady paychecks and risk everything to work 100 hours a week with the risk of not seeing any returns for a while for their passions.

Dear Luminary, you will know your business and center so intimately as you should in your first year or two. You will have details in your mind, compartmentalized that you can respond to any single moment that arises like an expert in everything. This is necessary for you to someday create the protocols and job descriptions you will need to do as you start to grow and need to allocate your responsibilities and roles. It will blow your mind as to how many roles you have played and need to resource out. This will be another incredible milestone and initiation in letting go of control and trusting others to show up in their zones of genius to contribute to these positions and roles in their unique and fresh ways under your guidance and model. You will be empowered to know who will thrive and succeed in the roles needed in your center. You will know this intimately as you have been every single role you are now hiring for and that's the reward for being a multi-dimensional multi-tasking multi-hat-wearing boss babe. These are the times where you will realize how much you are growing, embodying, and transforming.

On Setbacks, Failure and Even Tragedies

There's going to be failure. There's going to be setbacks. There's going to be discord between you and people. You will be responsible for a whole lot of things and sometimes the reflections you receive are hard to bear and look at. You will lose friends. You will be humbled in the ways you need to be. And sometimes, there's going to even be heart-breaking tragedies that no mindset can prepare you for. Don't be discouraged. Know that this too was contracted. These are the moments that test and initiate the leader within you. Paradigms can shift here instantly.

What I've learned through failures and tragedies, is how tenderized your heart becomes. It's as if you are given an entrance to sit right next to God and get a time-out from the regular world. These are what I call the Come to Buddha moments. These are the times, you strip down to your soul and you self-reflect. And you have the tough conversations you need to have. And you find all the exits you can find and you list all the reasons why you should give up. And you sit with those reasons. You can yell and throw tantrums and scream at the angels here. They get it. It is important to witness everything be unearthed within yourself and to be witnessed by your closest circle of human and non-human supporters. It is tough to be human and feel stripped of your powers and feel alone. These are the same dark nights of the soul you had before you even begun this journey in creating your vision into reality. When you enter these particular thresholds, know that this is your greatest culminating initiations as a leader to reach the next level.

The greatest leaders and Luminaries have failed more times that we can ever imagine. The more you fail and rise up, the deeper your capacity is to embody your greatness. Failure and tragedies tend to carve us out. It gets rid of all of the rocks in our proverbial bowls of light so we can be clearer and deeper vessels to hold light. The wisdom and medicine developed within these initiations are priceless. No MBA or book or master teacher can teach you these gems. These gems are cultivated from within. All I can offer for these moments is the encouragement to lean in more than ever. Step into the fire. This is a fire created for you. There will be help and support. And you are surrounded more than ever by legions of angels, ancestors, and guides in these moments, despite how lonely you may feel. These are the golden moments. You will hatch again soon.

This Is When You Start Fantasizing about Dropping Everything and Becoming a Zoologist

Why a zoologist? Because animals are embodiments of unconditional love and even the risk of being mauled by a hungry tiger seems less dangerous than the risk of being vulnerable to the daily heartbreaks and ego-deaths we will encounter. When we create, we enter a zone of chaos. Many moving parts and spinning Universes descend upon you at times, and as the leader of this creation, you must learn to be comfortable in this chaos and even learn to not only embrace it but thrive in it. Here are the ways you can set yourself up to thrive.

Pace Yourself

Being a fire horse in the Chinese zodiac, I tended to burn myself out through the process if I wasn't careful. One of my greatest lessons in the building of this center was to pace myself. There is a fine dance between pushing a project forward and being the fire that lights that drive and then letting it go and knowing when to pause, let things settle and practice patience waiting for alignment before moving forward. I know when I do it again and build, this will be the biggest change I will make. I will slow it way down. I will savor each step. I will trust in the natural progression of building that will make itself known.

Up-level Your Self-Care and Make it a Non-Negotiable

Another thing I would enhance when I co-create a retreat again is to up the self-care. The project will be no good, if you're exhausted.

You will be cranky and you will be unclear and unable to make wise and sound decisions, if your cup is empty. Remember you are the nucleus of this project and your well-being is pivotal in the success and flow of this endeavor. Decisions, small and large ones will always keep coming your way. Obstacles and challenges will continue to test you through each turn and growth of this project, practicing self-care and self-love will keep you strong and give you the stamina for the long haul. Create a schedule where self-care is a priority daily. Even if it's as simple as a five-minute meditation to begin your day. Create a schedule where you have one day per week, that is not scheduled and allow yourself to rest, adventure, clear your mind of agendas and goals and simply open yourself up to inspiration. Create moments to refuel yourself because creating a healing center and lifestyle is a marathon and not a sprint.

One Task at a Time & Celebrate Each Victory

Sometimes, you will finish one major project and aspect of the building of your center only to turn the page and find another seemingly endless list ahead of you. It can be overwhelming to take your blueprint and execute each step on your blueprint. This is when you must break down each major goal into small tasks. The joy of checking a box, even if it's as simple as weeding the spiral garden preparing it to be tilled, can be very satisfying. Celebrate these little moments and tasks accomplished. Although your GPS is always pointed to your North Star and destination, acknowledge the milestones along the way and make sure to celebrate them and the people that helped you and the project to get there. As I look back on our journey in creating this retreat center, the biggest mindset I would change is I would celebrate the little things more.

After all, they are just as important and are the integral building blocks of your center.

Trade in Expectations for Divine Collaborations

Expect nothing. There is another nuanced dance between setting clear intentions and not having expectations in how things will unfold. This is another Jedi Super Power that will take trial and error to really be able to alchemize. Expectations can derail your journey and fixate you on a path that debilitates your flexibility and muddles your clarity. Set your intentions and goals, see it clearly and when you embark upon the path toward these goals, be flexible and present to each step. If you need to pivot, not having expectations and attachments to how it *must* unfold, will make the pivoting and the flexibility so much easier and usher in more grace and peace in your world. Remember that this is a co-creation with the Divine. Always expect miracles and be in the question of *how much better it can get?* You'll be surprised at the imagination of God and how audacious your Co-Creator likes to get with the magic.

Meditation is the Greatest Super Power

One of the biggest ways to equip yourself as a leader of this incredible opportunity to create healing spaces in the world, is to begin each day or task with meditation. I find that the more I have to do in one day, the longer my meditation must be. Centeredness and cultivation of your Peace Muscle creates a crystal clarity and harmony between all levels of your being — the emotional, mental, spiritual and physical. As you continue to develop these calm expansive spaces within yourself, you are able find these spaces more easily throughout the day when twists and turns and sometimes surprises and challenges meet you. You are able to make the best decisions in these calm spaces and the relationship you cultivate with your Spirit is priceless.

Evening Recaps with Spirit

At the end of the day, when you are ready to wind down, one of the practices I find to be as helpful as starting the day with meditation, is ending the day with journaling. It's a nightly check-in I have with myself. I review the day. I note the lessons I've learned. I reflect upon how I could have done things better with more joy, with more presence, with more clarity, with more compassion. I write this without being critical of myself, but more with a tone of a mentor who's always cultivating your gifts and genius in a loving and compassionate way. I end the journaling session with gratitude. I think about what and who I am grateful for and I make sure to acknowledge my gratitude in writing. Sometimes, I write down questions I need help with and that is my love note to Ancestors and Spirit to help bring clarity and resolution into my dreamtime. After all, we are the most powerful in our dreams and we can affect our waking reality with the intentions we plant in our dreamtime. Book end your day with an evening ritual and intimate conversation with yourself.

Get Your Inspiration On

One of the greatest mind-hacks I practice often when I start to get overwhelmed or feel down (which is absolutely natural in the ebb and flow of creation) is I seek out inspiration. I read books, or listen to audible books these days especially when I'm traveling. I watch movies and documentaries, researching the lives of Luminaries I admire or researching creations I find beautiful and see how they were created. I go on adventures around the island

and play tourist in my own backyard, opening up my senses and awareness and let nature show me its genius and magnificence. I take cat naps which can be so rejuvenating and resetting, and dreams during naps are also different from dreams at night. I play with animals. I listen and dance to music. I remind myself to stay curious and open because you never know where inspiration and the muses will find you. Often, during the most mundane errand in town, I'll have a conversation with a stranger that will spark an idea or solution to something I'm navigating. God is in the details, corners and crevices of our days. Sometimes we have to remind ourselves to stay aware and soften to notice the genius and inspiration all around us.

There will be many moments in your journey, dear Luminary, when being a zoologist just seems like the most brilliant exit and escape in the world. Know that it's perfectly natural to feel this way. It's healthy to slow down, in fact it's necessary to. It's wise to meditate, rest and refuel. And it's important to celebrate the small victories as much as you celebrate the big ones. This will build your stamina; this will equip you with the drive and fuel for the long haul and remember that your Courage Muscle and Wisdom Muscle will get stronger and stronger when you can embrace failure as your greatest teacher. This is embodied spirituality and the journey of a new paradigm leader. It is equal parts grit and glory.

10: ROOT INTO JOY

*"Since the beginning of time, people have been trying to change
the world so that they can be happy. This hasn't ever worked,
because it approaches the problem backward.
What The Work gives us is a way to change the projector —
mind — rather than the projected.
It's like when there's a piece of lint on a projector's lens. We think
there's a flaw on the screen, and we try to change this person and
that person, whoever the flaw appears on next. But it's futile to
try to change the projected images. Once we realize where the
lint is, we can clear the lens itself. This is the end of suffering,
and the beginning of a little joy in paradise."*
~ Byron Katie ~

The Struggle Is Not Real

Your suffering is *very real*. I am not dismissing the very real pain we
feel as humans in our daily lives with the title of this section. There
is no spiritual bypassing happening here, as I've learned personally
the dangers of that when I've tried to use spiritual lessons to avoid
and deny pain and all the emotions that come with it. What this

title means is that the *struggle* which is our resistance to the reality that is happening in front of our faces, and in our minds, and in every cell of our being through every level of emotional, spiritual, and physical — that resistance is fear and that fear is illusionary.

Often times, if not every time we resist reality, we actually help perpetuate more of that particular reality. Eckhardt Tolle, the Luminary and author of *The Power of Now* and *The New Earth*, writes:

> *"All negativity is caused by an accumulation of psychological time and denial of the present. Unease, anxiety, tension, stress, worry — all forms of fear — are caused by too much future, and not enough presence. Guilt, regret, resentment, grievances, sadness, bitterness, and all forms of non-forgiveness are caused by too much past, and not enough presence."*

With that said if we were to show up very presently to our reality, in full vulnerability and readiness to feel everything, see everything, hear everything that the moment is bringing us, *especially* the pain if that is what's being presented – we'll find that it's so much less suffering in the end, if we can really face it and be present to everything that arises from that moment. It surfaces, we feel it, we learn from it, it expands us, it goes. Something else surfaces, we feel it, we learn from it, it expands us, it goes. And so on. This takes such discipline and intentional practice every single moment and it sucks, truly sucks but I promise it gets easier as you build your Presence Muscle. It will become your default replacing the habits of denial and fight or flight. You will struggle less and less because you will get used to opening up and surrendering to every moment of reality. Where there is no tension or resistance, there is no struggle.

This is one of the most important muscles you will use in the journey of creating your life work and healing center. Presence. Remember that it is your choice to struggle or not. You can be present to reality and all that it brings and can learn the lessons and initiate through the gauntlets now or have to repeat it over and over and over again. You cannot hide from your evolution. The game is not rigged against you that way. It is rigged for your success and highest alignment. The house (your Highest Self) always wins.

In this new paradigm existence, creating a healing center doesn't have to be on the vibration of struggle. Growing, expanding, learning, transforming doesn't have to be synonymous to suffering. We are learning to transform and grow through joy. In order to root ourselves in joy, we must be willing to face, be present to and digest all things that are not joy. Feel the pain and let it transform us. Don't resist the pain and prolong the struggle. One of my favorite modern-day philosopher poets, Nayyirah Waheed, writes, "Grieve. So that you can be free to feel something else."

The Attitude of Gratitude

Where thoughts go, energy follows. This is one of those hacks I go to when I'm feeling blocked, stuck, spiraling into doom and gloom. We all have those moments, and we will continue to have those moments no matter how evolved we are. There's always the next level of initiations and often times the initiations are initiations because it is a test of our embodiment. Life, for a Luminary especially, is always willing to up the ante on embodiment. Checking you. Elevating you. Making you more and more aware of your light and brilliance. So this is my go-to and number one consciousness hack when I'm down and out and struggling. Anything can be reframed with this question: how is this (fill in the blank) benefitting me? That's it. That's the abracadabra secret spell-breaking question.

It can be as light as finding the silver lining in literally a rain cloud. It can be as deep and difficult as finding a benefit from extreme abuse. Eventually, this Gratitude Muscle gets stronger too. And when we use it over and over and over again, neuropathways begin to form in our brains. And when we experience moments that challenge us, that cause pain, anxiety, sadness, anger – as we create space for those feelings and experience – it is much easier to find that neuropathway that automatically leads you to not only recognizing and being present to the pain but also recognizing and being present to why it's a blessing in your life and growth too.

The more we focus on what we are grateful for, most especially the moments where it's harder to find what we are grateful for, we quantumly shift reality. We infuse what we are grateful for with this energy, it activates happy neuro-chemicals in our brain showering our entire body with it, we shift in frequency and it not only transcends the moment and perhaps the extreme pain you are feeling, but it draws to you more of the resonating frequency. The Attitude of Gratitude is a big immunity boost. Put it in your medicine magic box and use it often.

If All Else Fails, Byron Katie That Shit (Don't Believe Everything You Think)

When a Luminary is about to realize a dream, there is almost an acceleration of challenges and initiations to really test you. The test can be surprising, depending on how clever our egos are. Our egos are masterful shapeshifters. I mean, I find myself having moments where I'm just in awe of my ego and how good she has gotten at shapeshifting. Her primary job after all is to keep me functioning in society. Keep me intact. Keep me solidified in my identity so I can keep bringing the bacon home so to speak. She loves her job and she has no plans on retiring, ever. So she has learned to character study me like her life depended on it … because in fact it does. She knows my insecurities (because she created them) like the back of her hand. She has memorized all of my experiences and has sticky notes on the experiences that caused me a lot of pain. Her role is to preserve me as best she can. She is preserving my heart and identities like a giant jar of pickles. And there is absolutely nothing "wrong" with that. Our egos are not our enemies, as some new age spiritual teachings make it seem. I have always found it much more joyful to have a loving relationship with my ego, establishing that my Spirit is the alpha leader here yet also appreciating the ways my ego helps me navigate the world and being the personality that shares the gifts of my soul. It helps to be amused by our egos too. They're like the neurotic parts of ourselves that get the job done. After the end of each day, they can sit in the nourishment of your soul's arms and express all of their neurosis and know we can witness them without succumbing to them.

I consider Byron Katie as the Joan of Arc of the mind. Her sword is The Work. The Work is the best lie detector on the market, in my opinion. I would definitely put this in your medicine magic bag. If you're familiar with The Work – isn't it profound? Keep using it. Don't let it get dusty. Don't get comfy. If you aren't familiar with The Work here are the four seminal questions to ask your beliefs and thoughts that are causing you suffering:

1. Is it true? (Yes or no; if no, go to question three)

2. Can you absolutely know that it's true?

3. How do you react, what happens, when you believe that thought? (What images do you see? What emotions or physical sensations arise as you witness those images? How did you treat the other person? How did you treat yourself? Do any obsessions or addictions begin to appear when you believe that thought?)

4. Who would you be without that thought? (How would you see or feel about the other person?)

Can you see what a powerful tool this can be in reframing the way we see things that are causing us suffering? "Without our stories," Byron Katie says, "we are not only able to act clearly and fearlessly; we are also a friend, a listener. We are people living happy lives. We are appreciation and gratitude that have become as natural as breath itself."

She goes on and suggests, "Happiness is the natural state for someone who knows that there's nothing to know and that we already have everything we need, right here now." If we can develop this Joy Muscle, we will be more fit in facing our thoughts and beliefs and the illusions of the blue pill popping world. That's the Happy Buddha. That's Jedi magic.

A mantra from Byron Katie's lexicon I love to remember whenever something happens that causes me anxiety is, "Everything happens for you, not to you. Everything happens at exactly the right moment, neither

too soon nor too late. You don't have to like it ... it's just easier if you do."
It's not just easier, but it can actually be more joyful.

String Theory and Alternate Universes May Be the Key to Ending Anxiety

On a Saturday morning in January of 2018, most of the residents in Hawai'i received this alert on their cell phones:

BALLISTIC MISSILE THREAT INBOUND TO HAWAII.
SEEK IMMEDIATE SHELTER.
THIS IS NOT A DRILL.

For thirty-eight minutes many believed there was a nuclear missile heading our way and life as we knew it may end. For many, there was absolute panic. The news reported on this panic, of course, and focused on it. Parents were throwing their children into potholes, believing it may save them. Families were gathering in bathrooms, in their bathtubs, just waiting for the missiles to come. My friend who was at a morning regatta for her daughter's paddling team ran with the masses toward Ala Moana mall, she recalled, for what, she wondered in hindsight. There were the lucky ones who slept in and never even knew what happened. Some folks were enjoying life without their cell phones on and also were spared the thirty-eight minutes of this apocalyptic simulation. I was in bed making love (if there was a nuclear apocalypse happening, I couldn't imagine a better way to go out, I guess) and we heard the alarms on our phones, but figured they were just flooding alarms (which we get a lot of here during the winter rainy season) and so we ignored them.

What was even more upsetting to me, personally, was the way the occupying government here in Hawai'i handled the situation. In the wake of everyone's trauma, they held a press conference blaming this older gentleman for "pressing the wrong button." Every part of my being – intuition, instincts, logic, emotional intelligence – everything just rolled their eyes *way* back.

There were so many theories that resulted from this event. Some folks felt it was a psy-op experiment by the military. Some folks felt that it really happened and it was intercepted. Some folks reported that they saw a blinding flash in the sky where the supposed interception happened. And then there are some folks who believed the missile hit. And it killed us all. And we just jumped timelines and a new similar Universe and life goes on. That last one caught my attention and interest.

I started to research string theory and one of the best videos of it is of this blonde freckled Dennis-the-Menace-looking twelve-year-old-prodigy quantum physicist. He's in college or perhaps even getting his PhD already in Quantum Mechanics and he explained string theory and multi-universes on a napkin as his father filmed him for YouTube. He proposes that CERN (the European Organization for Nuclear Research) altered some kind of molecule and catastrophically blew up our Universe a couple years ago. Say what, Dennis the Menace? He continued to speak so confidently and nonchalantly about our Universe ending, I totally bought it and went with it. He expressed how we simply, through string theory, just shift to the next "string"/Universe. More seamless than switching from HBO to Showtime on your TV, I imagined. He proposed that we don't even feel it. Sometimes, however, there are details about the last Universe that never made it through. And he continued his tutorial in his kitchen with his dad, but I paused the video and just really sat with that and all the feelings that started to arise from that.

I was so at peace with that teaching and possible reality. I thought, so CERN blew up our Universe and we're all still experiencing life as we knew it because we simply switched to the next Universe. Perhaps it was his delivery. And those freckles. And the napkin. I digested that really well and I immediately felt off the hook of any kind of anxiety ever. This became my own personal (have never shared this with others) anxiety hack. Sometimes the Armageddon agenda that is playing out in different world arenas really sends me into anxiety. Sometimes much more simple things like what a colleague might be judging me for sends me into anxiety. Either end of the spectrum, sometimes I'll envision this young boy, explaining string theory to me and I think, well, we'll just pop into the next Universe, it's okay, the world, my universe, literally *cannot* end. Somehow that soothes me. And if this doesn't help you at all, just throw it away.

I suppose I connect this to the notion that our souls are eternal and this experience we are having on earth in this particular time and space is such a tiny little blip and it really is about our soul's growth and what is innately *us*, our essence, our soul, our divinity, is truly indestructible. Even if molecules are altered. Even if missiles come. Even if you are getting divorced and you don't think your heart can survive it. You do. Your indestructible soul continues eternally growing, expanding, deepening in expression. It has helped my anxiety tremendously to have this parachute that lifts me up to suspend me in time and space so I can remember that perhaps this is all a simulation for our soul's evolution and that we are indestructible. Call it magical thinking. Call it basic string theory. It's my parachute during extreme moments that happened to have found itself in my medicine magic bag. I don't use it that often, but it's there and it feels good to know it is.

I tuck in this epic line by Ursula Le Guin in *The Farthest Shore* into my medicine magic bag, too: "I do not care what comes after; I have seen the dragons on the wind of morning." It just makes me feel like a Jedi warrior.

The Event Horizon

I attended the Cusp Conference in Chicago in 2018 and was inspired by all of these incredible Luminaries who were asked, "what keeps you up at night and what makes you spring out of bed in the morning?" One speaker, John Coyle, spoke about The Event Horizon. He was a former silver medalist Olympian in short track speed skating. And so he said, his life was all about time. The difference between a gold medal and the life that creates for you and no medal can be fractions of a second. He ended up studying time and becoming a leader in chronoception – the study of how humans process time. He let us all hold his silver medal as he told us about The Event Horizon.

He believes we can turn one hour into 10,000 years if we wanted to. The secret … you got it … *presence*. Full being presence. To create moments and experience moments with every cell of your physical being and every emotion as if you are savoring every millisecond. He says, children do this naturally. That's why summers seem so epic to them. He also says some people who are dying experience Event Horizon moments too. He quotes a man he studied who was given a month to live. This man began his memoir with, "I am blessed. I was given one month to live." This man created Event Horizon moments every day until he passed and he was determined to live life as if he lived to 100.

An Event Horizon moment is to cherish and be present to reality and show up to reality with every part of our awareness, to stay vulnerable to that reality, to feel the pain fully and deeply in that reality, so we can have room to also feel other feelings about it to as we digest them all, to practice gratitude of that reality. This is how we can time travel, John Coyle proposes. This is bending and stretching time.

In the creation of your healing center, there will be Event Horizon Moments. Make sure you recognize these moments and savor them. Stop the million and one things you are multi-tasking. And take it all in. Stretch it out. Experience it with every cell. Feel everything. This is an integral part of embodiment. It's an accelerator of our embodiment. Don't skip it for other things on your list. This will fuel those things on your list with more energy than you can ever imagine.

Less Judgment, More Fascination

I cannot recall when and why and how I started doing this but when I did start doing this, I noticed how considerably more joyful I became. When I felt like I was about to diagnose something or someone, or judge something or someone … I backspaced the words that were beginning to travel from my brain to my mouth, and instead I replaced it with F-A-S-C-I-N-A-T-I-N-G. Not in a sarcastic way either. Genuine fascination. Rather than feel irritated or assaulted or just plainly affected by someone's choice of actions or words, I stayed curious. Interesting decision I would think, huh, I wonder what his process is? It's an incredible shift. It's soft.

Allowing. And keeps the moment open to more insight and deeper awareness.

Children are great at this. They are fascinated with everything, eternally curious and can sometimes *why* you to exhaustion. My former wife and I started practicing this together after I shared with her my little hack one day. And it became really fun especially during moments where something would normally disturb our peace, and instead it transmutes the situation when we catch ourselves and both say out loud, "Wow, that's so fascinating!" And really mean it.

Often times, that reaction even surprises the person you are saying it too. We're so used to being judged. We're so used to slipping on that armor really quickly and have our defense ready. But what if we are just allowed the space and room to be our authentic selves without everyone quick to judge but rather just stay curious about the uniqueness that is us and how we grow and move in the world? When we respond with curiosity with each other, rather than immediate judgement, we call the essence and truth out gently from each other. We loosen our rigidity and our need to protect ourselves. And therefore, we begin to show up more vulnerably and authentically. That's an environment for more joy to enter. So be fascinated. Be in awe. Stay curious. Life can be such a wild adventure full of things that will surprisingly delight you.

If you can stay curious and fascinated throughout the entire process of creating your healing center ... I will fly to wherever you are and bow down and kiss your feet and hang with you and learn. Because that is self-mastery. I believe this is the key to joy. This is the key to success, too. We leave a lot of room for the Divine to show up in these situations and in each other when we remain curious and open. Stay in the question. Keep upping the question too. Dear Universe, please continue to fascinate me and bring me into delighted awe. If we keep asking for that, can you imagine the kind of realities we will start to create?

11: YOU ARE THE ONE YOU'VE BEEN WAITING FOR

*"You have been telling people that this is the Eleventh Hour,
now you must go back and tell the people that this is the Hour.
And there are things to be considered…*

Where are you living?
What are you doing?
What are your relationships?
Are you in right relation?
Where is your water?

Know your garden.
It is time to speak your truth.
Create your community.
Be good to each other.
And do not look outside yourself for your leader.

*Then he clasped his hands together, smiled, and said, 'This could
be a good time! There is a river flowing now very fast. It is so
great and swift that there are those who will be afraid.
They will try to hold on to the shore. They will feel they are
being torn apart and will suffer greatly. Know the river has its
destination. The elders say we must let go of the shore,
push off into the middle of the river, keep our eyes open,
and our heads above the water.*

*And I say, see who is in there with you and celebrate.
At this time in history, we are to take nothing personally,
least of all ourselves.
For the moment that we do, our spiritual growth
and journey come to a halt.*

*The time of the lone wolf is over. Gather yourselves! Banish the
word 'struggle' from your attitude and your vocabulary. All that
we do now must be done in a sacred manner and in celebration.*

We are the ones we've been waiting for.'"
~ Hopi Elder Prophecy ~

As I write this chapter, over 290 families are mourning the
loss of their loved ones who died in suicide bombings targeting
churches and luxury hotels on Easter Sunday in Sri Lanka. I just
read that Denmark's wealthiest man, billionaire fashion tycoon
Anders Holch Povlsen, and his wife Anne Storm Pedersen lost three
out of four of their children in the bombing. The article spoke of
the wealth of this couple and their plans of turning 200,000 acres

of the highlands in Scotland into a rewilding, reforesting landscape to preserve for future generations. The article didn't speak about the unimaginable heartbreak of this family in losing their children. I don't think that could ever be expressed in words anyways.

There's been a media blackout, but one doesn't have to read or see pictures; it is felt deep within the hearts of humanity. The majority of the people who died were in worship of the divine within themselves and each other and celebrating the Ascension of Jesus on Easter Sunday. The Agenda of Annihilation and Self-Destruction is unfolding in the world. Climate change, engineered environmental calamities, fracking, oil leaks, radiation leaks continue to create extreme and dangerous conditions causing typhoons, polar freezing weather, breakout forest fires, hurricanes, undrinkable water, extinction of animals, rapid dying of the coral reefs. There is an acceleration of death and destruction. If you tune into the news that really is all you see.

What isn't highlighted in the news is the accelerated awakening of humanity. The billions of people who are choosing to love one another, support one another, heal themselves, transform themselves and serve one another. The billion acts of kindness happening in one day is never highlighted in the media. Drama, sickness, and calamities sell in the old paradigm that was always rooted in fear to control the masses. In the new paradigm, everything that is created is rooted in *love* to *liberate* the masses. And that is where you and I come in.

As the Hopi Elder eloquently and potently shared:

"You have been telling the people that this is the Eleventh Hour, now you must go back and tell the people that this is the Hour. And there are things to be considered … Where are you living?

What are you doing? What are your relationships?
Are you in right relation?
Where is your water? Know your garden. It's time to speak your
Truth. Create your community. Be good to each other.
And do not look outside yourself for the leader."

This is the great calling drawing the Luminary in each of us out, to not only find a seat at the table, but create new tables, new healing centers, new organizations, new businesses that are rooted in love and designed to liberate one another into sovereign divine expressions of genius, kindness and inspiration. As we rebirth ourselves and our realities, we rewild and renew this earth with new forests, clean rivers and oceans, fresh air and renewed balance and harmony. This is an Earth School after all, and the school mirrors Her students.

Birthing a new paradigm, while leaving the old – exactly like the major transitions in our lives – in relationships, homes, careers, sickness, and deaths – can be a very chaotic time that's worsened if we resist it. The Hopi Elder says:

"This could be a good time! There is a river flow now very fast. It
is so great and swift that there are those who will be afraid. They
will try to hold on to the shore. They will feel they are torn apart
and will suffer greatly. Know the river has its destination. The
elders say we must let go of the shore, push off into the middle of
the river, keep our eyes open, and our heads above water. And I
say, see who is there with you and celebrate. At this time in history,
we are to take nothing personally. Least of all ourselves. For the
moment that we do, our spiritual growth and journey come to a
halt. The time for the lone wolf is over. Gather yourselves! Banish

*the word struggle from your attitude and your vocabulary. All that
we do now must be done in a sacred manner and in celebration.
We are the one's we've been waiting for."*

What an incredible invitation to not only surrender to the cosmic river of a new paradigm arising within each of us, but this instruction to *celebrate,* it is profound and that will make all the difference in our experience as we move through The Great Shift and create our offerings and services to our communities. What's more resonant to the New Earth? Ushering it in haggard and exhausted in shambles? Or ushering it in with gratitude, celebration, and excitement? The Authentic Embodied Luminary within you is ready to fully take part in this Great Shift. Your entire life and entire soul's journey has led to this zero point in time and space for you to use your gifts, genius and heart of service to usher in the new paradigm with others who are illuminating the world with you. Light it up! Now is the time. And the world has been waiting for you.

Strong Back, Soft Front, Wild Heart

Our idea of strong leadership is also deepening and liberating itself from the patriarchal definition and embodying in the genius of the matriarchal and divine feminine way. This way is nurturing, intuitive, magnetic, healing, courageously vulnerable and wildly free and fluid. When the divine feminine is married to the divine masculine which is confident yet humble, loyal in devotion, firm yet flexible, adventurous, strong yet gentle, it is a divine marriage within that transforms us into holistic embodiments of the divine leaders we were born to be.

Brené Brown's recent books *Braving the Wilderness* and *Dare to Lead* explore this new paradigm leadership. One of the mantras she repeats is taken from Joan Halifax and transformed as "Strong back, soft front, wild heart." According to Brené, this is the most ideal inner alignment for an effective Leader. Strong back is knowing yourself very clearly and knowing your boundaries and setting them very clearly. Having a strong back allows you to have a soft front, no armor needed, in any given situation and interaction. You are open because you know you've got your back. And therefore your heart can be courageously wild and lead you and your healing center, community, business, ministry and movement in the wise and inspired ways it was created to do.

What does a wild heart do? It loves unconditionally. It is of service to life. All life. And when it can be wild and vulnerably open, it will show up in its Highest Most Authentic Embodiment always. She says, "Vulnerability is the birthplace of innovation, creativity and change." That is the business we are in as Luminaries, envisioning and creating this new paradigm as we go. And we must dare to step into this arena, and fail and fall, and keep getting up. We will keep getting up because after all, our hearts are wild and our backs are strong.

You Come as One, but You Stand as 10,000

If you only knew the millions of miracles that created you and brought you to this moment ... If you only knew the millions of souls – ancestors, angels, ascended masters, star family, spirit guides – supporting you and waiting for you to invoke their help ... if you only knew of the prayers of millions of people all over the world asking for the gifts and medicine that you have to bless their lives and relieve their suffering … you would be emboldened and so grateful to show up for your leadership and your service.

Whenever I hear Maya Angelou's words, "I come as one, I stand as 10,000," I get chicken skin, tingles up and down my spine, and the hairs on my neck stand erect. That acknowledgment of all the unseen guidance, support, and prayers from all our unseen ancestors, angels, guides and fellow humans connects us to their fields of energy and magic. That's why we physically feel those chicken skin moments when we recognize how supported we are, when we invoke the help we need, when we need to be witnessed and we pray. Do not ever underestimate yourself. Do not ever feel lonely even in the moments where you are certain you are the only one that knows the lengths and depths in what it is taking to create this healing center and your offering to the world. You are witnessed and celebrated by so many.

If you believe in the spiral of time and that everything is actually happening simultaneously, then exponentially multiply these beings by 10,000 more as your descendants and the seven generations and beyond are also praying for you and supporting you. Your choices and faith to leap and build your wings on the way down, as Ray Bradbury coined, and be of service is causing a butterfly rippling effect through time and space. Not only are you shifting the lives of your ancestors, healing their pain and manifesting their dreams, you are also shifting the lives of your descendants. What an incredible opportunity and gift that is.

Your love is exponential as is the support you have cheering you on, praying you on and celebrating you. Remember this, especially during the times you are scared and feel alone.

Our Greatest Fear

One of the greatest (wo)manifestos of our time is Marianne Williamson's poem in *A Return to Love*. I will include this here so you have an all-in-one magic book of miracles and guidance whenever you need to tap in:

Our Deepest Fear
By Marianne Williamson

Our deepest fear is not that we are inadequate.
Our deepest fear is that we are powerful beyond measure.
It is our light, not our darkness
That most frightens us.

We ask ourselves
Who am I to be brilliant, gorgeous, talented, fabulous?
Actually, who are you not to be?
You are a child of God.

Your playing small
Does not serve the world.
There's nothing enlightened about shrinking
So that other people won't feel insecure around you.

We are all meant to shine,
As children do.
We were born to make manifest
The glory of God that is within us.

It's not just in some of us;
It's in everyone.

And as we let our own light shine,
We unconsciously give other people permission to do the same.
As we're liberated from our own fear,
Our presence automatically liberates others.

What else can I say, really? Don't you just want to walk out into the middle of a busy city and shine your light after reciting this (wo)manifesto? Just beam and share your gifts and ideas with the world? Stop folks on the street and reflect to them their genius and beauty and embodiment of love after reading this?

As I mentioned, I had the great privilege of seeing Marianne Williamson over one weekend in L.A. as she began her presidential run. She was such an inspiration and living embodiment of a leader. She exuded a humble confidence, the wisdom of an ancient sage, the humor of a goddess who knows exactly what she's talking about and doing and the compassion of a bodhisattva. She spoke greatly about the necessity to embody our spirituality and use our *light* to shine into what is dark, to surface what is dark and not look away, but examine it with all of our presence and faculty. She spoke of civil and political engagement as being the greatest way we can embody our spirituality, which is in the service of humanity, especially those who are suffering. She spoke of the necessity that America needed to reconcile with its shadow especially slavery and proposed legit reparations for African Americans. She is up-leveling spiritually and challenging us all to be more of service and be more engaged than ever. She too sees the Great Shift happening and feels the urgency to show up on levels she may not have ever imagined showing up when she first began her career as a spiritual teacher.

Leadership comes in many forms and are needed in many arenas. In the arena of healing, transformation and innovative creativity, a leader, in order to serve as many people as she can, must first believe in her capability, readiness and success. With our clients and guests, to be an effective healer, our only duty is to create the optimum space for the client to recognize their divinity and vitality – a return to love, a return to harmony and a return to peace within themselves. We must create that space and we must see it for them. We must see them a fully healthy and embodied divine being. That is our only responsibility. And of course, as we are all mirrors for one another, we must also do this for ourselves. We must create the optimal space within us so we can recognize our divinity and perfection. We must see ourselves as authentically embodied divine leaders. Because we are. We wouldn't be called to this path, if this wasn't the birthright we were handed before we were born. The light is within you, amp it up so that all can see from every direction of time and space.

'Eli 'Eli Kau Mai – Let Awe Possess Me

I often go to the crater and get as close to the goddess Pelehonuamea as I can. Before the eruptions, before the roads cracked and you could walk right up to the cliff overlooking Kīlauea Crater, I would visit Her daily in the early morning and bring coffee and my offerings, usually some tobacco, and I'd sit with her and just listen and talk to her about everything that I was navigating. Answers and guidance always came right away. A group of nenes would seemingly come out of the crater itself and fly overhead, squawk-ing, in perfect formation. A spider would show itself on an Ohia tree. A cloud would float above the crater and veil the horizon. A sprinkle of rain would suddenly move through. Rainbows would appear in the caldera and move toward the lava lake. Sometimes chanters would be there and you could hear them perched on cliffs, especially at dawn, when they were greeting the sun with their oli, prayer.

Now, after the eruptions and the roads getting giant sinkholes in it, we can no longer go right up to the cliff overlooking Kīlauea Crater. So instead, I visit Her at the Halema'uma'u Crater, perched upon the rock wall behind Volcano House. I often go at night now, as it is the least crowded and often I'm alone again so we can intimately talk. The beverage of choice this time is whiskey, the "Kīlauea Fashioned" as they continue to make for me even though it's no longer on the menu, with homemade ginger and Italian imported cherries. This is for celebratory occasions or for other not so celebratory occasions, like matters of the heart. I often visit Tūtū Pele with the excitement and relief when one visits their grandmother. You know you will receive nourishment, uncondi-tional love, and sage advice and sometimes some raw real talk if you need it.

Living next to this divine temple is such a privilege I do not take for granted. The Kanaka Maoli of this island have taught me the humility and reverence one must embody to live on this land and have the blessing to steward the land here. It is not permanent, and if she decides to create more land replacing the one you are on, then clean your home, prepare the land, open your doors, leave your offerings, and welcome her in. Welcome the transformation, welcome the rebirth. It is the most enlightened teachings I have ever come across on transformation, death and rebirth. The Hawaiians embody it here. And us newcomers, we learn. You can learn this exalted surrender with resistance or you can push off into the current and celebrate it. Tūtū Pele is going to be there at your door regardless to teach you about surrender.

The goddess Pelehonuamea – is not only a goddess, a fiercely compassionate teacher, a model for transformation and creation but She is also a *force*. A living, breathing, elemental force that can be felt, seen and embodied. As Kekuhi Keli'ikanaka'ole says in her interview about the volcanic eruptions last year in 2018:

"There is a force the Pele is very responsible for and that's the magnetic force of the earth. We feel that.

"I'm talking about the Pele as the element. Her primary form is lava, magma. And so when we think about the goddess, we don't think about an extra form outside of that. We see the form that we're seeing today on the news feeds or Facebook feeds. It's right there!

"It's creation right in the front of our faces. If we want to think of anything close to that, watch the birth of your child, watch the birth of your friend's child. I think that's the closest we can get to that form of Pele as a divinity. The goddess is an energy. The goddess is a resource."

'Eli 'Eli Kau Mai is a rejoicing and awe we feel on this island as we witness the sheer magnitude of this energy creating the newest earth in the world. With this New Earth, the inhabitants here and the world at large who feel this energy deeply are also being rebirthed into new humans. There is nowhere else we need to look, but right here, right at our feet, on the ashes that have fallen from the sky, to understand where we are and who we are at this precipice of evolution in this time.

Kekuhi Keli'ikanaka'ole goes on to say:

"We know the island is still going to produce new land for a long time. That's why, reframe the way we're thinking about the activity that's happening right now, reframe it! It's not a destruction. It's a creation.

"We don't even know when this is going to happen again, and of course we grieve the loss of houses and things, but just reframe our community's orientation to what it is that's really happening. Look! We're living right here and we're going to have stories to tell for the next one hundred years. Stories that we read in the Pele and Hi'iaka books now, those are the things that were happening in front of people's eyes. So what do we do? Let's write it down, let's journal, you guys. Everybody who has the opportunity to pick ash up from their windshield and go Oh my God, this was just made, and it just popped out of the earth not ten minutes ago. Write it down! Be the community geophysicist so that we have stories for our great grandchildren for the next 100 years. That's the benefit."

What incredible permission and inspiration, to stay wide awake and in awe of the Great Shift and birth of a New Earth happening in front of our very eyes. To write this down, to integrate it, to embody it and share it with the world and future generations.

The Kanaka'ole Family, here on the Big Island, are the most beloved family that share generously the wisdom of Pelehonuamea and the Hawaiian Spiritual and Cultural Traditions and most especially they model what divine embodiment is.

We are the ones we've been waiting for and we are the witnesses and actors of this Great Shift and Awakening. Take your place. Pay attention. Play your role with awe and fascination. Be the vessel of this energy of creation. The Pele is modeling what that means to us as she continues to vent, flow, and create New Earth for life to grow. Our capacity to create is this deep. Our capacity to grow new paradigms on new earth is this powerful. I invite you all to spend some time here in Volcano. Come humbled, come ready, come with the offering of your visions and service, and let the Pele infuse you with this creative force.

"Beyoncé Wasn't Built in a Day"

"Beyoncé wasn't built in a day" is a saying I saw on a t-shirt hanging at Book Soup in LAX. If they weren't all extra small, I would have bought them all. In hindsight, perhaps I should have bought them all and given them to every little girl, boy, nibbling (gender neutral term from adrienne maree brown) I know, so they can understand how one creates an empire and movement. It takes dedication, stamina and your big old heart to serve and uplift people. That is what drives Beyoncé. That is what drives the most successful Luminaries in the world. It is to serve. It is to embody divine grace and divine perfection. It is to use what broke you and turn it into medicine, art, healing, transformation and inspiration for others. It's grace and grit; it's heaven and earth.

I've been a fan of Beyoncé since she began. She had an air of focus, humility, discipline, intrigue, and power. When she married Jay-Z her star rose even higher. When Jay-Z broke their vows and broke her trust, she created "Lemonade," one of the best albums ever released, in my opinion. It was vulnerable and transparent about her pain, about her anger and grief and the way she brewed that all together as she rose in her empowerment and liberation. It was not only spiritually rooted in the Orisha traditions and in its homage to the goddess Oshun and Black Girl Magic, it was rooted in the modern-day spiritual embodiments of every single woman who loves, who has her heart broken, and who rises from the ashes like no one's business.

Her lyrics were (wo)manifestos. Her lyrics could be sung walking down the street with a bat smashing windshields as she did in her video, yet they can also be sung in church and get the congregation up on their feet. She created a movement of empowerment for women and for African Americans and Black people around the world. She not only made lemonade, but she made the nectar of the gods from lemons. She broke, she raged, she grieved, she healed, she transformed, she reconciled, and she created babies, a renewed marriage, and an empire – all for the world to see. She made her Luminary Journey into art and empowerment.

Her greatest contribution that I am witnessing is the Beehive or sometimes called the Beyhive. It's her fans, her community, her family, her supporters, her team ... she devotes herself to them as a queen bee does. Her offering and service to humanity is palpably felt when she's on stage. Even if you're way in the back, her heart, love and belief in you connects to you through her lyrics and most especially through the way she's embodying it on stage and her waking life. She brings everyone up with her.

Her recent documentary she made is called *Homecoming*. It's on Netflix. If you haven't watched it, watch it. You will see a woman who spent eight months preparing day and night, night and day, just after giving birth to twins, while running an empire with her husband – she spent eight months preparing for a two-hour performance at Coachella. We know she's a Virgo, but damn. It was an incredible inspiration and also reality check to see how much accountability, responsibility, focus, passion, purpose and intention she puts in her offering to her fans, all to empower people to live their best lives. She says in the documentary, "If my country ass can do it, anyone can."

As Marianne Williamson writes:

"A queen is wise. She has earned her serenity, not having had it bestowed on her but having passed her tests. She has suffered and grown more beautiful because of it. She has proved she can hold her kingdom together. She has become its vision. She cares deeply about something bigger than herself. She rules with authentic power."

Own your wisdom and serenity because you have passed your tests. You have earned it. Grow to be more beautiful because of it. Become the vision of your healing center. Serve something bigger than you. Lead with authentic power.

12: BE IT AND THEY WILL COME

"Since the tapestry of all time has already been woven, everything I could ever want to happen in my life already exists in that infinite, nonphysical plane. My only task is to expand my earthly self enough to let it into this realm. So if there's something I desire, the idea isn't to go out and get it but to expand my own consciousness to allow universal energy to bring it into my reality here."
~ Anita Moorjani ~

Flow with It

We have covered a lot of ground here, dear Luminary. And the theme of *authentic embodiment* has been the backbone of every milestone we find ourselves at. You may have noticed that a majority of the challenges I address that may come up in this journey, are the ones that we manufacture from within. It may manifest itself in broken contracts, extremely delayed completion dates, a controlling investor, an unseen pivot in plans, an angry contractor, theft. These challenges are all meant to support you and all part of the divine contract you have with Life. The breakdown or the breakthrough highly depends upon the way you show up for it. Strong back, open front, wild heart? Courageously vulnerable? In awe? In gratitude? Curious? In service to life?

This Great Mystery School that you've entered because you said *yes* to embodying your light, to creating a healing center, to serving the world – it will ask everything of you. And it will, in turn, give you everything you need. In fact, it's already been given. It's been inside of you all along. And the gatekeepers, the challenges and the initiations along your journey they were placed there so that you can realize this amazing secret, that's actually not a secret at all and the sages have been telling us this all along, including the people who love us and see us. What a fascinating Earth gig huh? What an incredible privilege and opportunity to awaken, embody and be devoted to the divine within ourselves and each other in this way – as a Luminary, shining light across all space and time, creating spaces where others will also embody their light and share it with others.

Savor It

You didn't just come to Earth for the snacks. Not in this time, at least. The Great Shift? I mean, you're a cosmic baller. Even if it took you a minute to realize that, the bravest of the brave are here on Earth right now. You are amongst the Luminaries of the Universe, ready to light it up. Creating a healing center is a grand adventure of your life. Be present to what you learn. Savor the moments and create as many event horizons as you can. When you look back and watch the movie of your life, make the middle part, where all the action is happening, make that the most exciting and inspiring.

Invoke all the tears and all the laughter. Squeeze the moments with delight.

You have learned here different tools you can place in your medicine magic box, so that you can use them when a moment or challenge or question needs some levity and space to breathe – to make room for miracles. You have learned how to bend time and time travel. You have learned how to reframe even the most rigid and sure beliefs and programs. The growth you experience will be exponential. Similar to how plants grow. You wait and wait and wait, you water and you sun and you see nothing but soil. And then one day when you least expect it, and maybe even forgot about it, a little sprout pops up. And you rejoice! It's alive and it wants to grow and the conditions must be right! You walk away and the next day, it's practically a full-blown plant. Some plants just grow like that, especially when the foundational soil was prepared with a lot of intention and care. The moment you sprout to the moment you are a full on the leader of a healing center will flash by so quickly. So savor it. Savor the moments you are picking out the exact kind of doorknob you want from hundreds. There is God in those details too. Your unfolding is treasured and witnessed as the most precious thing in the Universe to all those concerned.

The greatest way to savor the moment is to enjoy it and be in the vibration of gratitude. Everything in life is a blessing when you realize everything in life exists for your highest and most exquisite evolution. The deepest pain is our closest friend and teacher. Joy is contagious. And Joy creates more joy, it multiplies quickly than any other emotion, because the frequency of it is so *light*. As Gay Hendricks says:

"Your capacity expands in small increments each time you consciously let yourself enjoy the money you have, the love you feel, and the creativity you are expressing in the world. As that capacity for enjoyment expands, so does your financial abundance, the love you feel, and the creativity you express."

Own It

I've had many different coaches in my life, in sports, my spiritual journey, my business and in love. Some of them may not have seen themselves as coaches and mentors, but I always saw them as one. Other people's embodiment of the qualities I strived to amplify within myself is the most inspiring thing about other humans. Everyone has such a unique embodiment, with a unique wisdom and a unique way of delivery that is their frequency and theirs alone. I love learning from other Luminaries. I love discovering their secrets and what they have in their medicine magic box. The very best mentors and coaches never take credit for what they've taught me either. For a winning game, or a well-executed retreat or a successful season in business or an amazing breakthrough in my relationship – they always say, "it's all you, boo" – in their own ways.

And so, I say that here. *It's all you, boo.* The spark of light was given to you. You said yes. You bravely took on the mission. You are slaying your fears. You're meeting your challenges and showing up strong back, soft front, wild heart. You're taking an idea, a mere thought and vision and you are practicing the greatest alchemy known to humankind, and that is the alchemy of manifesting a thought into a tangible reality on Earth. Not just any tangible reality, but one that creates space for healing, transformation, and inspiration for more love to express itself on Earth. You devoted yourself to humanity. In this process, you've had to be so honest with yourself and slay any kind of manufactured illusion, external and especially internal, to pass the initiations given to you, so you can be a vessel for this kind of co-creation and light. You are becoming a new human on this New Earth. Ingesting ashes. Processing the grief, anger, rage and all the feels of an old paradigm crumbling, externally and internally. From these ashes you rise and you generously share your new embodiment with the world. That's all you, Boo. No one else did that for you. You had support, yes. But no one, can embody what you've agreed to embody but you. So, own it.

The Invitation

This is your invitation. As the Hopi Elder said, "the time of the lone wolf is over ... All that we do now must be done in a sacred manner and in celebration." I invite you to join the pack of Luminaries and leaders – it's going to take all of us, working, creating, celebrating together not only to dismantle the old paradigm, but in building the new one, one sacred transformation and initiation at a time. To be witnessed in all of our courageous vulnerability and to bear witness to one another and cheer each other on is everything. It makes all the difference. It will be the reason why you'll get back up again after an epic fall. It's because we are holding each other accountable and we are reflecting, without any shame, the beauty of all of our cracks and broken parts to one another and saying, look how much stronger we are?! Look how much more beautiful?! And look at all that space for more light?! This kind of authentic embodiment is magnetic. If you become your whole self, unapologetically you, it will empower many who are looking for the same reflection and sometimes, permission. And they will come from all ends of the world to ignite their inner-light from yours.

Don't do this alone, dear Luminary. Don't do this in the dark. And you certainly don't have to do this and struggle. Reach out to all the other awakening Luminaries in this world and let's co-create this new paradigm together. The new paradigm is a tapestry of light intersecting, sparking one another, and creating new patterns and designs we have yet to imagine. These will be the solutions and insights we will need to resolve what has been broken, lay what cannot be repaired to rest and create new systems of harmonic resonance in all aspects of our realities — economic, social, political, agricultural, medical, educational … everything is up for a paradigm shift. This is our earth mission. It will take each one of us seeing our own genius and gifts and audaciously sharing it with the world. We've got to let go and let God, and flow with the cosmic river accelerating through this Great Shift. We've got to savor these moments of spark, innovation and creation. And we've got to start owning our sovereignty, beauty and light. This is a free will reality, so this is an invitation to the most epic celebration of all time.

I once had a dream when I was living in Manitou Springs, Colorado, that shifted my paradigm on the spot. It was during my nomadic days, healing my heart and apprenticing under healers. In my dream I was late for a party and entered this glass mansion in the Garden of the Gods, which is a majestic land covered in red rock formations in Colorado Springs. I was making my way through these all-glass hallways, trying to find the ballroom. I opened the gigantic doors to see everyone I knew, every human I've ever met and most especially my family — past, present and future. Everyone was dressed to the nines. And the minute I walked in they turned around from their celebrations, conversations and libations and started clapping. I was suddenly overwhelmed by tears of gratitude and joy. It was as if I arrived from a really long journey and everyone was waiting for me to celebrate with them. I woke up soaked in tears and buzzing with divine love, that's really the best way I can describe the essence of what I felt. There are a few ways to interpret this dream. For me, I visited another dimension where we are all embodied gods and goddesses in this glass house in our garden, calling our human selves home. And all it takes to get to this place is the recognition of the divine beings that we are.

13: THE PHOENIX RISES

"We are volcanoes. When we women offer our experience as our truth, as human truth, all the maps change.
There are new mountains."
~ Ursula Le Guin ~

One day I was scrolling through social media and I saw a poem an artist named Doris Varga had written:

Women
walk through fire
and build
healing centers
from ashes.

It ignited me. I looked around the café and thought, is she here? Is this poet here? Inconspicuously writing this poem for me to see? I saw no one that looked like they just posted this at the café. Could Spirit have orchestrated this moment?

I had no idea what I was going to write about when I agreed to write and be a vessel for this book. I was woken up at 12:34 a.m., I noted the numbers and thought, well there's got to be some aligned reason to be woken up at this time. And so I just laid there and listened. I suddenly got the inspiration and guidance to create a book cover. A book cover? It's 12:30 a.m. *Create the book cover*, said the Waker Upper. So I did. It took about fifteen minutes and it was two images of lava and gold (two separate images with the same symbols on it). The symbols were of a lotus, an egg, a butterfly and spirals in different shapes.

The moment I finished the "book cover" the words "Holy Ashes" typed across the image. Although, this didn't end up being the title of the book, it described the essence of the book perfectly and became the title of the second chapter. And I thought, "Wow. That's beautiful." I tried to put the phone away and thought I'd go back to sleep, but then I got another urge to keep looking at it and while I kept looking at it, I started to get the instructions that I'm about to write a book about transformation and embodiment in the ushering in of a new paradigm. It would be about what I experienced here. It would be about the volcano and the eruption and the New Earth. I got more information about how it was going to tie into a program I had been thinking about for a couple years I was calling "Luminaries in Residence." It was an offering I knew would be the most important offering we would have here at the healing center. And I was waiting for a clear sign from the Universe to initiate the idea. I was so excited that I was beginning to see the connection of this book to this program, I couldn't sleep the rest of the night.

That morning, I was suddenly again urged to just pitch the book to Angela Lauria and The Author Incubator. I wrote it and didn't even know what was coming out of my fingers. Yes, I pitched a book and my program (that just made itself known to me a mere three hours prior) on my phone. I had an appointment soon after

I finished typing it with my two thumbs (as I share this story, the audacity I had really just surprises me right now) and so I sent it off without even re-reading it or spell checking. Gasp! If my former writing teachers, editors, and journalist friends were in the room, someone surely would have tackled me before I could press send. I've come to realize that God is audacious. She does not care about typos and your perfectionism rooted in fear. God just wants you to be an open instrument for divine love and to generously share it with the world.

I wasn't sure what else this book was really going to be about until I started writing. And what I'm realizing is that the thread that runs through all of these chapters is one simple message. And that is you are divine, through and through. You are light. And the purpose of this offering to you is to bear witness to what is already within you and to inspire you and invoke you to share it and let that seed of light out. Let it shine bolder and brighter than ever before.

The purpose of this offering is to gather the magic and the potential miracles waiting to manifest from these pages. Do you know how powerful that can be? The words here that you have opened and unleashed are vibrating with that sacred whisper of potential. The potential that they enter your consciousness and a knowingness within you ignites. And suddenly you can see much clearer than you've ever seen, your divinity. The fire warms you from inside out and it burns night and day, waiting for you to sit with it and listen. The potential continues to unfurl itself into your consciousness. As a divine being becoming more and more aware of and intimate with Herself, what could want to be created? Expressed? Illuminated with your divine light?

That poem showed me myself, my journey, my transformation, the way I burned, and the way I rose and what I created from all of it. In those few lines, it did all of that. It illuminated the medicine and magic I carry. And it inspired me to not keep that to myself, but to share it as honestly and generously as I could. Because there is someone out there waiting to hear it. Waiting for a sign to begin, to accept the mission, to embrace the vision and to create their biggest gift and offering for healing and transformation of the world. We are constantly whispering to each other back and forth through time and space, urging each other to keep shining our light. That's what this is all about.

You are not alone. If you've let go of the rocks and pushed yourself out into this rushing river, and you have managed to keep your head above water, then look around. We are all here bobbing up and down with you. We are creating this new reality with you. We are embodying our higher selves with you. We are slaying the fear dragons. We are re-writing destinies because we can. Because we realized that's what gods and goddesses in human forms do.

In the *Spell of the Sensuous*, David Abram writes:

"There are so many unsung heroines and heroes at this
broken moment in our collective story, so many courageous
persons who, unbeknownst to themselves, are holding together
the world by their resolute love or contagious joy.
Although I do not know your names,
I can feel you out there."

I can not only feel you out there, I can hear you and I can see you by the frequency of the love you emit.

We need the healing centers you will be creating on this earth more than ever to anchor in the light and frequencies necessary to continue to make anything that isn't of love, obsolete, and continue to create everything that is of love flourish and serve the world for its healing, transformation and liberation.

I mahalo you, dear Luminary, for walking such a heroic path to be here. Let's anoint each other with the ashes we have scraped from our own journeys. I recognize and receive your truth, light and wisdom and mahalo for receiving mine. I mahalo you for your willingness to shine. Arkan Lushwala, an Andean ceremonial leader, who has written *The Time of the Jaguar* and *Deer Thunder* shared of a word *yuyay* during an interview with the Pachamama Alliance called "Indigenous Ways of Restoring the World." Yuyay means:

> *"To listen, to be humble; to be open to receiving;*
> *to pray in a way that invites the sacred; to look inside;*
> *to source wisdom from the seeds, sun, and water;*
> *and ultimately, to remember the universal intelligence*
> *that resides in each one of us as Earth-people."*

This is what we are being called to do. Each one of us has an incredible gift to share and a role to play in this incredible time in history.

O Ka Pono Ke Hana, 'Ia A Iho Mai Na Lani. Continue to do good, until the heavens come down on you. As an Auntie passed away during the writing of this book, we spent a lot of time in the hospice with her. We savored every moment we had with her. And engaged with her in her final hours, listening to every whisper she shared. The night of her passing was the most gorgeous sunset I think I've ever seen here on the island. It was so stunning, that it seemed like everyone was posting pictures of it from all around the island. No filters necessary, it was absolutely stunning and had every imaginable color known on Earth and beyond. My little nephew, my Auntie's grandson, he noticed the sunset first and he kept saying, "There's Grandma, there's Grandma." He insisted that his mom take pictures of it on her phone. That night she passed. Her husband wrote to the children and sent his photos of the sunset, and said, "The heavens sure did open up for your mama."

That morning, when I heard about her passing, a friend who was born and raised here on the Big Island, but now living across the ocean, randomly sent me this saying, O Ka Pono Ke Hana, 'Ia A Iho Mai Na Lani. Continue to do good, until the heavens come down on you. And in that moment I realized, we do not go to heaven, heaven comes to us. More accurately, heaven comes *through* us. Either in death or while we are still living. Heaven comes through us. That's what the sunset showed me. In the silences of my day, in prayer, often asking for help and clarity, I have begun to see heaven bridging to earth through the embodiment of our spirituality and humanity.

To honor Auntie's life, the whole family visited the Keauhou Watershed and Bird Sanctuary just across from the craters here in Volcano. And we were given the remarkable opportunity to plant over forty Koa Trees. Auntie was a water protector, a geologist that loved the sea and the rivers and knew how to hook a fishing line and throw it like no other. Planting a canopy of Koa Trees is to ensure a forest that can protect the waters that come down from the sky and find their way to the rivers and aquifers so that the future generations will be able to nourish and cleanse themselves with pure and fresh water. We put our prayers into the trees. We put our intentions into these trees. One by one, we planted them. Heaven manifests itself on earth in these simple and profound acts.

Tupac Shakur is one of my favorite poets, philosophers and modern-day prophets of our time and he once said, "I'm not saying I'm gonna change the world, but I guarantee that I will spark the brain that will change the world." That line has always struck with me since I was a teenager. He was planting trees, he will never be able to sit under. I know that if I continue to share resources with and create spaces for Luminaries to gather, discover their divine genius and launch their visions into reality, there will be inventions, movements, discoveries that will heal our oceans, earth, people and collective consciousness. These realities are pulling me forward to embody my own divinity as vulnerably and bravely as I can.

May what you create, dear Luminary, be a reflection of the embodiment of the Spirit and human that you are. May it butterfly ripple through space and time and may you feel, hear and know the celebration of all who witness you and support you. May they receive clearly your whisper of love manifested in form. May they be empowered to create their own legacy of love because of it.

ACKNOWLEDGMENTS

I mahalo and salamat the gatekeepers who taught me where my shadows lay and emboldened me to shine my light on them. It wasn't pretty, and even painful at times, but I'm all the stronger and gentler because of it.

I thank every lover and partner I have had the honor to love and receive love from. More than any humans, you have been the most potent portal of transformation for me, through my heart.

To Kahanu Fung, thank you for loving me as vulnerably and authentically as you did and letting go when it was time to let go. Mahalo for loving this ʻāina as deeply as you did and for the music, art, beauty and healing you shared.

To Frederick Grissom for being our first contractor here and giving us your genius and heart in the foundations of this home.

To Divona Cox for your altruistic generosity and investment of love and resources in this vision.

To Jeff Sarver for the tender warrior heart you shared with us before you transitioned here on the land. You are honored here every day by the way you've inspired us to infuse love into everything we do.

I thank all of my teachers and mentors who guided me in my spiritual awakening and gently yet firmly told me to go back down the mountain and practice what I've learned and most especially serve other people with all my heart. Salamat for all of the wisdom you have shared with me so generously.

I thank all of the aunties and uncles, builders, gardeners, healers, chefs, temple keepers, excavators, web designers, branders, marketers, financial consultants, clairvoyant guides, wisdom keepers, students and fellow Luminaries for co-creating this healing retreat center with me and most especially for going through the experience of healing and transformation we journeyed through together with every milestone. It is a continued honor to walk side by side with you all.

I thank Angela Lauria and The Author Incubator Team for midwifing this book into reality and shifting my paradigm with so much love, hillarity and practical magic.

I thank Reneau Kennedy, for infusing this book journey with so much enthusiasm and generously supporting me to launch.

I thank my Chicago homegirls, Vivienne Tan, Bridget Johnson, Victoria Chi and Joelle Belmonte, for making high school not only bearable but such a wild and beautiful adventure of self-discovery. Thank you for keeping it real all of the time.

I thank my Columbia College Chicago mentors, teachers and fellow writers, for being my comrades as I discovered my voice and experienced the healing power of storytelling.

I thank my Babaylan sisters and kapatids, for the medicine and love you embrace me in and lift me up with. I would not have agreed to this Earth Walk without you. Let us gather under full moons until our last breaths. And for our sister, Gigi Miranda, our wild Ancestor in the stars, salamat for igniting our fires with your life.

I thank this ʻāina that has brought me home to myself and continues to teach me how to live in humility, gratitude and service to this earth. This is the closest I will be to heaven.

I thank the people of these sovereign islands who live, breathe and walk *aloha* and who have humbled me in witnessing what that level of fierce love feels like embodied.

I thank my creators, Mom and Dad, Juan and Zen, for my life and the generous and unconditional wisdom and love you have nourished me with. Salamat for taking bold and fearless leaps with your lives and encouraging me to follow my dreams.

I thank my Family for always seeing my visions with me and believing in them.

I thank my Ancestors, who through space and time have helped usher in miracle after miracle to bring me to where I am today.

I thank my future descendants for calling me through time and space to step toward my destiny and do my part in perpetuating and creating heaven on earth.

I bow down to Pelehonuamea, for calling me to this ʻāina and teaching me the magic of fire, the exquisiteness of transformation and healing and the power of limitless creation.

I salamat God for conjuring up this evolutionary existence so we can discover the divinity within ourselves — what a genius creation– thank you for entrusting me with this wild life.

May my life continue to show all of you my gratitude as love in action.

ABOUT THE AUTHOR

DARSHAN MENDOZA is the spiritual director of Akuahā, a healing retreat in Volcano, Hawai'i. She curates personalized journeys of healing, transformation, and visionary incubation for her guests and clients for planetary transformation. In 2019, she launches The Luminary Journey, a new-moon-to-new-moon program and residency, where Luminaries birth their visions in a holistic and embodied way into the world.

Darshan was born in Manila, Philippines and moved to Chicago with her family at the age of seven. She graduated from the University of Illinois Urbana-Champaign with a BA in political science and minors in English and philosophy. She explored the world of law as a student at the John Marshall Law School and the world of creative writing at Columbia College Chicago. She worked as a paralegal, journalist and editor before her spontaneous Kundalini Awakening which led her onto a Healer's Path.

Soon enough the Ancestors of Hawai'i called Darshan to The Big Island where she began an accelerated decade-long Mystery School where she learned from wisdom keepers from the Philippines, Hawai'i, India, Tibet, the Black Foot and Navajo Nations, Burkina Faso, Nigeria, Mexico, Japan, China, New Zealand, the Bioenergetics Quantum Field, and the Kundalini Yoga and Meditation Lineage. The simplest way to describe Darshan is that of a visionary, healer, and teacher. She is committed to anchor in heaven on earth by creating healing centers, visionary incubation labs, schools and eco-villages all over the world and supporting Luminaries in discovering their genius and sharing it with the world. She finds home in Hawai'i, Chicago, and the Philippines.

Website: www.akuaha.com and www.TheLuminaryJourney.com
Email: darshan@akuaha.com
FB: Darshan Mendoza & Akuaha Hawaii
IG: Akuaha Hawaii

ABOUT DIFFERENCE PRESS

Difference Press is the exclusive publishing arm of The Author Incubator, an educational company for entrepreneurs — including life coaches, healers, consultants, and community leaders — looking for a comprehensive solution to get their books written, published, and promoted. Its founder, Dr. Angela Lauria, has been bringing to life the literary ventures of hundreds of authors-in-transformation since 1994.

A boutique-style self-publishing service for clients of The Author Incubator, Difference Press boasts a fair and easy-to-understand profit structure, low-priced author copies, and author-friendly contract terms. Most importantly, all of our #incubatedauthors maintain ownership of their copyright at all times.

Let's Start a Movement with Your Message

In a market where hundreds of thousands of books are published every year and are never heard from again, The Author Incubator is different. Not only do all Difference Press books reach Amazon bestseller status, but all of our authors are actively changing lives and making a difference.

Since launching in 2013, we've served over 500 authors who came to us with an idea for a book and were able to write it and get it self-published in less than 6 months. In addition, more than 100 of those books were picked up by traditional publishers and are now available in bookstores. We do this by selecting the highest quality and highest potential applicants for our future programs.

Our program doesn't only teach you how to write a book — our team of coaches, developmental editors, copy editors, art directors, and marketing experts incubate you from having a book idea to being a published, bestselling author, ensuring that the book you create can actually make a difference in the world. Then we give you the training you need to use your book to make the difference in the world, or to create a business out of serving your readers.

Are You Ready to Make a Difference?

You've seen other people make a difference with a book. Now it's your turn. If you are ready to stop watching and start taking massive action, go to http://theauthorincubator.com/apply/.

"Yes, I'm ready!"

OTHER BOOKS BY DIFFERENCE PRESS

About Face: Wash Your Face, Change Your Life, Tell Everyone by Emily Borja

Clothes the Deal: The Guide for Transformative Personal Style by Jenn Mapp Bressan

Your Dream Dental Practice: Happy Patients, Fewer Hours, Easier Life by Christine Curtis

Refuse Diabetes: 9 Steps to Holistic Healing for Type II and Pre-Diabetes by Teri Dale

Wake Up!: Break the Generational Cycle and Be Yourself by Janet Sellers Ellis

Own Your Brilliance: Overcome Impostor Syndrome for Career Success by Michelle M. Gomez

Shine: A Mom's Guide to Help Her Daughter Find and Follow Her Dreams by Neisha Hernandez

Pain Is Not What It Seems: The Guide to Understanding and Healing from Chronic Pain and Suffering by Anita Hunt Hickey M.D.

Goodbye, Comfort Food: How to Free Yourself from Overeating by Robin Rae Morris

Fertility Fuel: Create Your Family Without Losing Your Mind, Your Marriage, or Your Money by Susan G. Schiff

Alpha Bitch to Enchantress: Awaken Your Feminine Superpowers by Suki Sohn

The Art of Performing Powerful Presentations: The Executive Woman's Guide to the Magic of Inspirational Speaking by Natalie Venturi

The Uncherished Wife: Recover from the Emotionally Absent Man by Christina Vazquez

THANK YOU

And so we part for now, dear Luminary. As the Hawaiians say, a hui hou. Until we meet again. Salamat, mahalo, thank you, from the bottom of my heart, for receiving this offering and opening up a space in your heart for these words and stories to land. Little do you know how intimately I feel that I know you. In the solitary moments of composing this book, it was just you and me. As a gesture of my gratitude and wish to support and expand our network of Luminaries, I offer you this secret passcode: LOVE IS THE KEY. If you write to me at darshan@akuaha.com with this passcode in the subject line, I'll offer you a free Luminary Journey Consultation. It would be an absolute honor to hear about what led you to this book, what you are envisioning to create in this world and how we may support you in your journey. Let's light up this world together!

Luminaries in Residence

The Luminary Journey and Luminaries in Residence is a new-moon-to-new-moon virtual incubation and in-house residency designed to create space for healing, transformation, nourishment and inspiration for Luminaries like yourself. The goal is to launch your ideas into the world while immersed in a holistically curated program and retreat.

For more details and to apply please visit **TheLuminary Journey.com**.